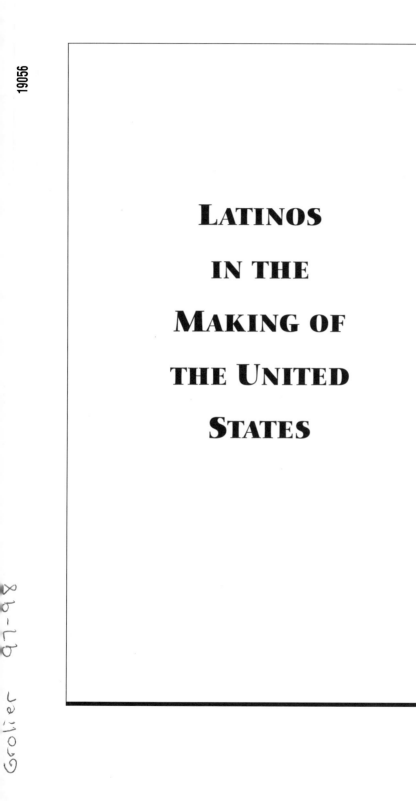

LATINOS IN THE MAKING OF THE UNITED STATES

James D. Cockcroft

LATINOS

IN THE

MAKING OF

THE UNITED

STATES

The Hispanic Experience in the Americas

Franklin Watts
New York—Chicago—London—Toronto—Sydney

For "Dr. Ben," who cares

Photographs copyright ©: UPI/Bettmann: pp. 23, 30, 33, 37, 39, 71, 120, 121; The Bettmann Archive: pp. 24, 141; Archive Photos: pp. 27, 53 (Consolidated Stock), 66 (American Stock), 78, 79; AP/Wide World Photos: pp. 51, 99, 130, 147, 158; North Wind Picture Archives, Alfred, Me.: pp. 62, 65.

Library of Congress Cataloging-in-Publication Data

Cockcroft, James D.
    Latinos in the making of the United States / James D. Cockcroft.
      p. cm. — (The Hispanic experience in the Americas)
    Includes bibliographical references and index.
    ISBN 0-531-11209-8
    1. Hispanic Americans. 2. Hispanic Americans—History.
[1. Hispanic Americans—History.] I. Title. II. Series.
E184.S75C64 1995
973'.00468—dc20   94-23933
                                                          CIP AC

CONTENTS

ACKNOWLEDGMENTS

I want to thank pioneers and friends in the research and teaching of Latino contributions to the making of the United States—writers like Edna Acosta-Belén, Rodolfo Acuña, Ernesto Galarza, Richard Griswold del Castillo, Jorge Klor de Alva, Carey McWilliams, and Virginia Sánchez Korrol.

For her many insights into the "hidden history" of our multicultural society, I thank writer and best friend Hedda Garza. No acknowledgments would be complete without recognizing the generous assistance of librarians and staff at Glens Falls' Crandall Library and SUNY-Albany's Library in New York State.

LATINOS
IN THE
MAKING OF
THE UNITED
STATES

INTRODUCTION

The word "making" is an energetic word, evoking mental pictures of people absorbed in physical work, muscles straining, faces glistening with perspiration. Synonyms for it include "building," "creating," "fabricating," "fashioning," and "manufacturing," in other words, "productive labor." When we speak of "making" a nation, we often imagine crews of people erecting bridges, roads, buildings of all sorts, and installing electrical and telephone lines. Without these visible structures, we have a barren desert or luxuriant forest landscape, but surely not a "nation."

Democracy can be another important component of nation building, but it is often undefined. We usually think of it as "freedom"—mainly freedom of speech and religion. But perhaps even more important is what President Franklin Delano Roosevelt called "freedom from want," the right to an adequate income. That starts with access to jobs, but includes the assurance of government assistance for those unable to find work. Workplace democracy means the right to organize a union and the right to a decent work life. Educational democracy means equal access to quality schools, where all students are treated with respect and given an equal chance to learn.

Mexican Americans, Puerto Ricans, Dominicans, Cubans, Central Americans, South Americans—all so-called Hispanics[1] or Latinos—have brought their working hands and all of their skills and talents to the United States, contributing enormously to the making of this nation. Their participation in this process has been largely ignored, mostly because of racist stereotyping—pigeonholing groups under false, negative labels. Many people think of Latinos (and African Americans) strictly as manual laborers and servants—"mere" ditch diggers, gardeners, and maids.

Nothing could be further from the truth—or so insulting to people who work primarily with their hands! In this book, we will reveal the indispensable role of Latinos in *all* areas of making the United States.

First, introductions are in order. Latinos come from many places and are the nation's fastest-growing "minority."[2] By the year 2015, if current population trends continue, they will outnumber African Americans. According to the 1990 census, 22.4 million Latinos live in the United States. Estimates range up to 5 million Latinos who were not counted, however. Also not included were 3.5 million Puerto Rican American citizens living in Puerto Rico.

At the time of the 1990 census, Latinos were living in many areas of the nation. A third of the Latinos could be found in California; a fifth in Texas; and a tenth in New York. Florida is home to 7 percent of all Latinos and there are also large concentrations of Latinos in Illinois, New Jersey, Arizona, New Mexico, and Colorado, in that order.

Most Latinos live in cities because that's where most work is to be found. Los Angeles is home to about 5 million Latinos; New York City, 3 million; Miami, 1 million; and San Francisco, Chicago, and Houston each have close to 1 million Latino residents. Thirty other smaller cities are each home to more than 100,000 Latinos.[3]

Latinos, like every other ethnic and racial group (excluding Native Americans) in the United States, are originally from someplace else. In numerical order, the largest group of Latinos, 64 percent, originated in Mexico; 13.7 percent are from countries in Central and South America; 10.5 percent are from Puerto Rico; 4.8 percent Cuba; and the census counts "other Hispanics" as 6.9 percent. Counting estimated "illegals,"[4] immigrants from the Dominican Republic today outnumber Cuban Americans (a million or more). Half of the Mexicans have been here four generations or more, many of them coming during the "great migration" of 1890–1930, when an eighth of Mexico's people came here.[5]

Like the other immigrant workers throughout history, Latinos have been significant "producers" in the making of the United States. Coast to coast they have left the mark of their architectural skills everywhere. Latinos' skills in the United States have been fundamental for the development of the mining, forestry, railroad, construction, ranching, and food producing and processing industries. As operatives in manufacturing, Latinos have helped develop the modern textile, garment, furniture, and electronics industries, as well as sectors of heavy industry, such as steel. New York could not have become the garment capital of the world in the 1950s and 1960s without Puerto Rican workers. The nation's garment industry today, facing stiffer competition from overseas, would collapse without the Dominicans and other Latinos it employs. Latinos are also the key labor force for many restaurants, hotels, and other services.[6]

Central to the nation's early industrialization was the power of electricity. Electrical power generation and distribution depends on copper, a mineral noted for its high electrical conductivity. In the peak industrializing years of 1890 through 1929, when the United States produced more than half the world's copper, mines in Arizona generated nearly half of that total. The mines were developed and worked mainly by Mexicans and Mexican Americans (see chapter 3).[7]

Copper is also noted for its high thermal conductivity, making it important for coolant systems in automobiles, refrigerators, and air conditioners, as well as numerous apparatuses used in the chemical industry and others. In retrospect, we can now appreciate that Mexican copper miners, known for their world-class skills, were essential to making the United States an industrial giant.

Miners and other workers had to be fed. Without the agricultural labor of Mexicans, Puerto Ricans, and other Latinos, there would not have been enough fruits, vegetables, poultry, and meat to feed the nation's growing population of immigrants that helped the nation industrialize. In 1932, when Mexican workers were being deported by the tens of thousands as scapegoats for the nation's 25 percent unemployment rate, the head of the U.S. Department of Agriculture informed the public that the Mexicans "have helped so much to develop this country . . . their absence will be sharply felt by all those persons who employ workers in large numbers."[8]

If electricity, copper, and food were so important for the country's industrialization, so were the railroads. Without transportation, it would have been impossible to connect the mines and farm fields to the cities and markets across the land or to coast ports. There ships stood ready to take U.S. products to the rest of the world, establishing the United States as an important partner in world trade. In the nineteenth-century West, where copper, coal, and gold mining and agricultural production developed rapidly, Mexicans and Mexican Americans accounted for 70 percent of the section gangs on the main railroads.[9]

Today, Latinos are as crucial as ever for the future of this country. In cities such as Los Angeles, Chicago, and New York, Latino workers are helping to keep manufacturing from leaving the area, saving the declining manufacturing sector from a complete collapse. As low-paid service workers they are helping to revitalize several fading downtown areas. Their low-paid labor in highly competitive wholesale and retail marketing, as well as in the finance, insurance, and real estate industries, is infusing "new life" into the nation's struggling cities.[10]

Categories devised by the U.S. Bureau of the Census for the labor force are rather general, but they still give some idea of all the jobs Latinos do. Latinos are engaged in basic service and production work at about twice the rate of non-Latinos. Nearly half the nation's Latinos work at blue-collar jobs as operatives, fabricators, and laborers in manufacturing, broadly defined. About a fourth are employed in white-collar occupations—managerial, professional, administrative, technical, sales, clerical—only half the percentage of non-Latinos. A fifth of Latinos work in services, particularly health, food, hotel, restaurant, and household services. The remainder, under 5 percent, work in agriculture or other areas.[11]

The public (government) sector is the nation's largest employer, but Latinos are not well represented there except at the local level, where they are as numerous as whites. In local governments they are employed largely as low-paid clerks or in other service jobs, such as sanitation, janitorial services, and the like. Cuban Americans, for reasons made clear in chapters 5 and 6, are economically better off than most other Latinos. More of them are white-collar (office) workers.

The professional jobs like teaching, law, and medicine almost always require a college education and an advanced degree. Although Latinos remain underrepresented in the colleges and therefore in these fields, they are playing an increasing role in the professions. In the business world, too, where educational qualifications are not always necessary but large financial investments are needed, there have been almost no Latinos until recently. Now a handful have become store owners, bankers, and factory owners. And although grossly underrepresented in politics, some are major political leaders as well (see chapters 2, 4, and 5).[12]

A nation without culture is scarcely a nation. Culture, broadly defined, includes literature, art, the media, music, cuisine, and, of course, sports. Latinos have created an exciting body of literature, as well as numerous new magazines, newspapers, and television and radio stations and programs. Some have achieved prominence as artists, actors, musicians, composers, and dancers. They are important players in the national pastime of baseball, as well as other sports. Latino foods and music are widely appreciated.[13]

No nation can progress if its people suffer from ill health and high infant and adult mortality rates. A "civilized" country must be able to point with pride to excellence in preventive medicine and care for the sick. Latinos have been generally shut out of the highest-paying medical professions, those requiring many expensive years of training, but they have contributed enormously in all the other echelons of health care (see chapter 2).

Perhaps the least recognized contributions of Latinos have been in the making of democracy. Often the victims of racist violence and undemocratic practices, Latinos have been key actors in the union movement and in the ongoing battle for better schools. They have a long and distinguished record of participation in the struggle for civil rights and human rights (see chapters 3, 4, and 6).

It is often said that "immigrants made America." Today Latino immigrant workers are needed more than ever. A group of them informed this writer in 1981 that "the employers tell us, 'Come, don't stop coming, you are the ones who get the job done—if you don't come, we'll lose everything.'"[14]

In times of economic decline, or "recession," there is always a dangerous resurgence of "nativism" (anti-immigrant behavior and blaming immigrants for unemployment). Recently, Latino immigrants have suffered the brunt of this scapegoating. They go on building America, but under increasingly unfair conditions.

In the pages that follow, we will see how vital all Latinos are to the nation's very existence—and why it is so important that the class, race, and gender obstacles they face be removed as soon as possible.

1
uno

THE

FARMWORKERS

We are important because of the work we do.
We are human beings who sweat and sacrifice,
bring food to the tables of millions and millions
of people across America and around the
world.
— Cesar Chavez,
United Farm Workers leader, 1986

Long before the "Grapes of Wrath" had
ripened in California's vineyards a people lived
on highways, under trees or tents, in shacks or
railroad sections, picking crops, cultivating
sugar beets, building railroads and dams,
making barren land fertile for new crops and
greater riches.
— Luisa Moreno, Spanish-Speaking
Peoples Congress founder, 1940

Is this the best way we can grow our big orchards?
Is this the best way we can grow our good fruit?
To fall like dry leaves and rot on the topsoil,
And be known by no name except deportee.
— "Deportee," lyrics of folksong by
Woody Guthrie[1]

Imagine almost any American family's holiday meal. The festive table is decked out with delicious-looking foods, wines, and juices—an awesome variety not to be seen anywhere else in the world. The main dish may be a turkey, a roast beef, a ham, a salmon, or some other kind of specially prepared poultry, meat, or fish. Steaming hot in side dishes are string beans, asparagus, artichokes, carrots, Brussels sprouts, broccoli, cauliflower, beets, corn, potatoes, or other nutritious vegetables. Salads made with several kinds of lettuce, tomatoes, cucumbers, pickles, carrots, onions, scallions, and parsley are piled high in wooden bowls. Others overflow with succulent strawberries, oranges, melons, peaches, cherries, apples, pears, and plums. Close by are several varieties of nuts—pecans, walnuts, peanuts, pistachios. Even the desserts and coffees arrayed on a side table or in the kitchen sport a variety of choice ingredients: pecan pie, apple pie, peach pie, strawberry shortcake, layer cakes, and puddings with amaretto, chocolate, light, dark, even decaffeinated coffees.

Few people at the holiday table think of the source of all this wonderful food. Even when we go to the supermarket and see it so beautifully displayed, we rarely stop and ask ourselves: Where did all of this come from? How is it that Americans have more food and in greater variety than any other people on earth?

Of course, the food industry workers produced this abundance from start to finish; yet few of us can imagine the difficult and skilled nature of their efforts. Some food workers live overseas, picking and sorting coffee beans in Colombia or Brazil, cutting sugar cane in the Dominican Republic or Central America, harvesting cashew nuts in Africa. But most live right here, working at the nation's farms and food-processing and meat- and poultry-packing plants.

On one of the nation's mega-acre farms, you can glimpse the labors of those who produce and clean the food we eat. Along rows of crops as far as the eye can see, you will spot clusters of people bending over and moving hurriedly along. They are men, women, children, entire families, picking the vegetables. A twin-engine plane roars low over a neighboring field, dusting the crop with a foul-smelling pesticide. You instinctively cover your mouth with a handkerchief to block out the windswept fumes.

Nearby are more people, usually women, working at long tables, sorting the crop by size and quality as it passes along a conveyor belt. Farther away may be canneries, tin-roofed factories filled with the noise of machines and the steam of huge vats. More people work there. And if you wander farther down the road and look carefully, you will spot the dormitory shacks where the workers are housed, primitive facilities with only one outhouse. Or, looking deeper through the trees, you may see the hovels and shacks migrant farmworkers have built along the riverbed or under a bridge. Some live with no roof at all, sleeping under trees.

You may be struck by how poor and how young so many of the workers appear to be. That's because less than half the nation's farmworkers receive the minimum wage—so low today it buys 30 percent less than it did in 1968. More than a third of all farmworkers are under seventeen years of age. Most are Mexican. They are known as the poorest of America's workers. Yet they are the ones on whom we depend the most! They and some of their ancestors helped build what is known today as modern agriculture.

Technological innovations also helped. Because of air freight and refrigerated railway cars and trucks, highly perishable foods can be provided year-round. Many of the "winter vegetables" we eat are imported from Mexico. "Out-of-season" fresh-picked strawberries come from the Mexican state of Michoacán.

It all started long ago. As the country's population grew between 1776 and 1880, more food had to be produced. When 24 million immigrants arrived between 1880 and 1920 to help the country industrialize, our numbers doubled and there were millions of additional mouths to feed. The introduction of sophisticated farm machinery and the consolidation of large farms revolutionized food production.

Modern agribusiness got its start, as food production became a big business. For the rest of the twentieth century, the small family farm was unable to keep up with the costs of new machines and the competition of gigantic corporations like Del Monte, Ralston Purina, and Tenneco Oil Company. With each new economic downturn, more farm mortgages were called in, until today hardly any family farms are left at all. Today's big corporations of "agro-industry" set the pace.

But expensive machines and wealthy agro-industrialists could not do it alone. Machines could not cut, harvest, or pick crops like strawberries or tomatoes without crushing them. Millions of pairs of hands were needed to set out the tender baby plants called seedlings; weed and cultivate around their delicate roots as they grew; pick, sort, and handle them at harvesttime—always careful not to bruise them. As the growers' needs for workers to do this skilled but strenuous work grew, they turned to the impoverished population of Mexico for help. Over the years, the majority of our nation's farmworkers were Mexicans brought into the fields of California, Texas, and other states.

Actually, the Mexicans had been in the Southwest long before all this happened. Today's Texas, California, and other western states belonged to Mexico until the United States invaded that country in 1846. After the U.S. victory in the Mexican-American war, the 1848 Treaty of Guadalupe Hidalgo and 1854 Gadsden Purchase brought nearly half of Mexico's territory under U.S. control. It included the valuable gold, copper, water, and other resources of today's Southwest. The war left a bitter legacy, since numerous atrocities were committed by the Americans, repeating a pattern established in the earlier takeover of Texas.[2]

The more than 100,000 Mexicans of the conquered territories had built up the Southwest in the centuries before the war. In the 1800s they had taught their skills to newly arriving English-speaking "pioneers." But the English-speaking settlers in Texas were not very grateful. Many called the Mexicans nasty names like "greasers." This was one way bigoted people made Mexicans appear "less than human" to justify taking their lands and going on occasional lynching sprees.[3]

The Mexicans' special skills not only in agriculture but also in mining (see chapter 3) helped build the America we know today. Skilled Mexican-American shepherds and shearers helped develop the booming sheep-raising industry—often on lands they once owned! Cattle ranching started with Mexican *vaqueros* (cowboys), who introduced the invading "Anglos" to the skills of the saddle, bit, bridle, spurs, lasso, and bronco-busting. One scholar later wrote: "The only original traits of the Anglo cowboy were his swaggering attitude and his predilection for killing Indians and Mexicans."[4]

Mexicans helped spawn the citrus and cotton agro-industries that sprang up along the shores of rivers in Texas, Arizona, and California. Men, women, and children helped develop, sow, and harvest new plants and crops, giving rise to the nation's food industry—everything from vegetables to fruits and nuts. For example, Texas's pecan industry and California's walnut industry became multimillion-dollar businesses, while the Mexicans who picked, shelled, and canned the nuts lived from hand to mouth. Mexican sugar beet workers helped augment Colorado and Kansas production fourfold from 1900 to 1910. African Americans, poor whites, and other workers from the Caribbean and Latin America also worked in agriculture, mostly along the eastern seaboard.

Work and housing conditions in the fields were so wretched that Mexicans often tried to escape and go back home. Consequently, some growers kept "their" Mexicans handcuffed at night. When they needed more workers to harvest their crops, the owners obtained the federal government's help. For example, in 1909 the United States signed a treaty with Mexico guaranteeing a thousand Mexicans to harvest California's sugar beet fields.

Not only were more working hands needed if America were to feed itself, but they had to be available on short notice to meet seasonal demands for different crops. Once a crop was in, there was no longer any use for them. As a result, *migrant workers* became the nation's agricultural labor force, to be hired and fired according to seasonal needs.

In 1924, the U.S. Border Patrol, the country's only national police force, was created to make sure a kind of "revolving border door" system worked smoothly at the 2,000-mile-long border between Mexico and the United States. The border's door swung to the north to import Mexican farmworkers when they were needed and to the south as soon as the crops were in. Standing near the door were labor recruiters to welcome the arrivals and load them onto trucks. Next to them stood border patrol guards ready to deport them after the harvest—or *before* that if they tried to form a union! A corrupt system of bribes and payoffs made millions of dollars for employers, labor recruiters (known as *enganchadores* or *coyotes*), and lawmen, while stripping the immigrants of their last *centavos* (pennies). The system continues today.

During World War I, when there was a labor shortage because of Americans going off to fight in Europe, employers got the government to open the border door extra wide. The government even lifted the immigration law's eight-dollar head tax and literacy tests to let Mexican workers through the door. In the early 1920s, cotton growers' associations imported tens of thousands of Mexicans. They still do.[5]

For generations, Mexican families worked from sunup to sundown in the cotton fields, helping ultimately to clothe America. Until the introduction of synthetic fibers, almost

An agent of the INS Border Patrol questions a migrant worker while a Border Patrol plane flies overhead.

*A mounted Border Patrol unit near El Paso, Texas.
The Border Patrol was created to police the
Mexican-U.S. border and facilitate the process of
the "revolving door" of Mexican immigration.*

all clothing was made from cotton or wool. After the cotton was picked it went to nearby cotton gins for processing. Then it went to New England's textile mills where female immigrants from Europe wove it into fabrics. Finally, Italian, Jewish, and other garment workers in New York City's man- ufacturing "sweatshops" worked the fabrics into the pants, shirts, skirts, and dresses that clothed America. Puerto Ricans in the 1920s and Dominicans in the 1960s began obtaining these sweatshop jobs too, at least in New York, while Mexicans and Central Americans entered the appar- el industry in the Southwest.

In the sunbaked fields of Texas and California, Mexican teenagers stumbled under sacks of cotton weigh- ing them down. One cotton picker in the 1950s, a father of small children, later recalled how he was paid $2.50 for a 100-pound sack, not enough to meet his food and rent costs unless he worked extra fast. Picking cotton often left his fingers bleeding and his back painfully stiff. The check paid him at the end of the harvest typically left off the final week of pay. There was little he could do about it. Using his gnarled hands to demonstrate, he described the work he did for most of his life:

> *To pick cotton you have to lift up—pick not like this but like this—and get to the dry part here in the middle. Then, you and your workmates are lining up like this, all the way up to your waist in cotton, and you are grabbing with this finger while the other is right behind picking. And someone else is right behind you, and then the next guy, right? . . . I was, quite frankly, completely exhausted and worn out from having to work so hard to come up with the money to support my children.* [6]

From early times farmworkers tried to organize themselves to win decent wages, the right to a union, better treatment— usually without outside help. For example, in 1903 Mexican farmworkers united with Japanese immigrants to win an agreement with farm owners in Ventura and Oxnard, California, to employ only union labor.[7]

In the 1910s and early 1920s, when they were helped by the multiracial Industrial Workers of the World (IWW—"Wobblies"), farmworkers, most of them Mexicans, formed a large union called the Agricultural Workers Organization.[8] However, their strikes, together with those of Mexican miners crucial to the copper industry, led to a series of nativist attacks on Mexicans known as "brown scares." Violent deportations, the jailing of IWW leaders, and tougher immigration laws, including a prohibition against public medical assistance for immigrants who had been in the country less than five years, left Mexican farmworkers still struggling to survive. After that, they experienced a vicious cycle of trying to organize unions, followed by economic recessions, followed by outbreaks of anti-Mexican violence scapegoating them for unemployment problems beyond their control. For example, their 1928 cantaloupe strike in California was followed by the 1929 stock market crash and more deportations.[9]

During the Great Depression of the 1930s, farmworkers kept feeding America. They also maintained their struggle to unionize. They could count on little outside help. In urban America, people were caught up in strike waves and factory sit-ins of their own. Labor unions rarely sent organizers to rural areas the way they did to the textile, garment, automotive, rubber, and steel plants (see chapter 3).

Nonetheless, thousands of Mexican and Mexican American strikers unified with other farmworkers in melon, lettuce, and strawberry strikes that sometimes won them union contracts. One historian later described the battles against lawmen and hired thugs of the corporate growers as "an all-out war."[10] Determined never to turn back, farm and food industry workers went on to launch more strikes that by 1938 brought tens of thousands into their union movement. Walkouts by thousands of mostly Latina can-

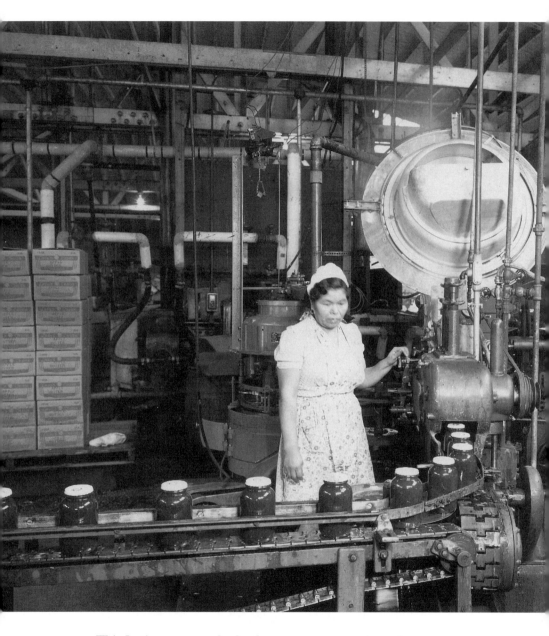

This Latina woman checks the conveyor system in a plant that produces bottled apple butter. Latinas are a major part of the workforce of the agricultural industry.

nery workers further lifted people's hopes that at last they would win a decent wage.[11]

Relatives of Latino agricultural and cannery workers in steel and other industries in the Midwest joined the giant strikes and factory sit-ins that finally forced the government to pass laws guaranteeing the eight-hour workday and the right to collective bargaining between unions and employers. But farmworkers were generally exempted from the new laws. In the end, they could not withstand the employers' superior force of the state militia and the use of other desperate unemployed people to break their strikes and unions. To most Americans, farmworkers remained "invisible."

Even the occasional publicity given to farmworkers' wretched lives of near starvation, such as John Steinbeck's prize-winning 1939 novel *The Grapes of Wrath*, completely overlooked the Mexicans. Steinbeck wrote about the poor white "Okies" fleeing the Dust Bowl of greater Oklahoma in the late 1930s.[12] In fact, Dust Bowl refugees often replaced striking Mexican farmworkers, as happened in Santa Paula, California, in 1941. Later in the 1940s, when many of the Okies "made it" out of rural poverty by taking up factory jobs, the Mexican farmworkers were left behind, as "invisible" as ever.

When the United States entered World War II in 1942, the need for Mexican workers grew so intense that the United States signed a treaty with Mexico called the Bracero Program (*bracero*, from the Spanish *brazo*, or arm, means "working hand"). The bracero treaty authorized the use of contract labor (which had been outlawed in 1886) to make up for a labor shortage caused by 14 million U.S. workers going off to fight the war.

After the war, the Bracero Program was extended and the braceros helped create today's highly profitable agribusiness. Until the program's end in 1965, as many as half a million braceros entered the country *each year*. Modern agribusiness could never have developed without them.

Through its "supplemental agreements," the 1942 treaty with Mexico supposedly protected the braceros' rights, but in fact they were appallingly abused. The U.S. Labor Department executive who oversaw the program from 1959 until its demise later described it as "legalized slavery."[13]

A bracero who made dozens of trips in those years described the large number of deaths and what the work was like:

> *Ay, what an exhausting job, to go along an endless row . . . hoeing, cultivating, weeding. We used* el cortito, *a six-inch short-handled hoe [banned as inhumane by California governor Jerry Brown in 1975], and bent over like this, all the way stooped over, to make for sure weedless lettuce. . . . In the evenings I would unbend myself and see my face flabby with fat and my hands swollen because all the blood had rushed downward.*[14]

To add insult to injury, in 1954 a government-orchestrated program called Operation Wetback was introduced. In eighteen months nearly *1.5 million* Mexicans were deported! The aim was to scapegoat them for the economic recession that occurred after the end of the 1950–1953 Korean War and to destroy the National Farm Labor Union that had organized a series of "wetback strikes." The humiliating term "wetback" was introduced to denigrate immigrants crossing the treacherous waters of the Rio Grande. It was applied then as today to almost all Mexicans, Central Americans, and even Mexican Americans.[15]

Some of Operation Wetback's deportees were Latino U.S. citizens caught up in the nationwide dragnet. Other deportees were braceros, here legally. Yet even during Operation Wetback the border door revolved to the north faster than ever, as employers brought in hundreds of thousands of fresh nonunion workers.

Meanwhile, the U.S. government encouraged more Puerto Ricans, technically American citizens (see chapter 3),

*Under "Operation Wetback" these Mexicans
looking for work were taken off a freight
train by the Los Angeles police.*

to come to the United States. Between 1944 and 1960, the island government organized the outmigration of a third of the island's population—a million people—mostly to the East Coast. It was a key part of a new industrialization and antipoverty strategy called Operation Bootstrap. Many of the new arrivals were jobless *jíbaros* (peasants), but about half were skilled or semiskilled factory workers who fanned out to cities like New York, Chicago, and Milwaukee. They faced intense racial discrimination and were relegated to the lowest echelons of industrial, service, and agricultural labor. From Florida to New England, some of the Puerto Ricans worked in the harvesting and canning of fruits and vegetables. Today these contract farm laborers are known as "commuter" migrants. Each year 20,000 of them arrive, follow the "harvest trail," and then return home. They too feed America.[16]

Today mainland Puerto Ricans are the nation's second largest Hispanic group. They, like Mexican Americans and other Latinos, have helped build up various manufacturing industries, especially in clothing. They also have worked as low-paid help in hospitals (see chapter 2), restaurants, hotels, and private homes. Without them, the restaurant, tourism, garment, and food industries would not have been able to expand after World War II.

None of the huge profits flowing from agribusiness's steady growth were spent to give Latino farmworkers decent houses or better medical care. If they and their children were to "make it in America," they would have to do it themselves, as they had always done. No one was going to come and do it for them.

There were a few who, despite their exhaustion at the end of the day, thought of what to do, of how to make the fields a better place to work in, free from dangerous pesticides like DDT and unsanitary, unsafe dormitory rooms rented to them by the growers. From among those few came the future leaders of the first lasting farmworkers' union, the United Farm Workers (UFW), founded in 1962.

Some of those who grew up in the fields and moved to the cities vowed not to forget their "roots" but to go back to organize their people to win a better life.

Among them were UFW organizers Dolores Huerta, Cesar Chavez, and Tony Orendain. Daughter of a farmworker and a waitress, Huerta was a skilled organizer and a fantastic speaker. Chavez and Orendain had grown up picking crops in the fields and attending many different schools as their families moved along the harvest trail. Chavez became the first Hispanic to gain national prominence. Like Martin Luther King, Jr., he advocated nonviolence. To protest the murders, beatings, and jailings of pro-union farmworkers, he engaged in several well-publicized fasts.[17]

One of the farmworkers' most important victories was the winning of a ban on DDT. It was an important first step in the modern environmentalist movement. In 1966, the UFW won an historic first union contract with the Schenley Corporation. But the other big growers in Delano, California, producers of half the world's table grapes, held out. So the UFW organized a consumers' boycott of nonunion grapes and the beverages made from them.

In the big cities, people who cared about the civil rights of African Americans in the deep South and the lives of soldiers dying in Vietnam or of Vietnamese children napalmed by U.S. aircraft (see chapter 6) soon heard about the boycott. As they entered supermarkets and liquor stores, they saw grape boycott pickets and stopped at literature tables to pick up information leaflets. Many refused to buy grapes once they knew about the new farmworkers' support movement. Some spoke with local store managers and told them how to order UFW-picked grapes. Soon shopkeepers were posting the red-and-black emblem of the UFW at fruit and wine counters.

Chavez later acknowledged that the farmworkers might *never* have gained public attention if he had not gone to the University of California-Berkeley campus in 1965 and asked

*Cesar Chavez was one of the founders of the first
successful farmworkers' union, the United Farm
Workers (UFW).* Huelga *is the Spanish word for
strike. The UFW logo hangs on the wall.*

for help in the grape boycott. The students were some of the first to picket stores stocking nonunion grape products.

The UFW also conducted several long marches to draw attention to *la causa* (the cause). In Texas, Orendain and others led a march on the state capitol to publicize the Rio Grande Valley "great melon strike" of 1966–1967. Television cameras rolled as exhausted families made their way down hot, dusty roads and informed viewers about the subhuman living conditions of farmworkers. Only the heartless continued to buy non-UFW products.

Once again, desperate growers approached the government. The U.S. Defense Department helped them by buying nonunion grapes and shipping them off to the soldiers in Vietnam. Returning vets described how sick and tired they were of grapes![18]

The boycott spread. By 1969, 17 million adult Americans refused to buy a single bunch of grapes, forcing all the grape growers to settle with the UFW. New contracts banned the use of five deadly pesticides, including DDT, even before the federal government acted.

To keep up the momentum, the UFW launched a lettuce boycott to help win another hard-fought strike. In 1975, the nation's first legislation recognizing the rights of farmworkers was passed, California's Agricultural Labor Relations Act. It was a victory not only for organized labor but for all Latinos, since until the UFW made headlines they were an "invisible minority."

But as the border door kept revolving, and as new generations of children were born with birth defects from pesticides supposedly milder than the banned chemicals, the nation's agricultural workers faced new battles ahead. After the 1973 recession, the economy went into a tailspin. By 1994, the average wage purchased far less than it had two decades earlier. To try to revive the stagnating economy and regain their accustomed profits, employers began importing additional Mexican workers. That pool of cheap labor was augmented by more than 2 million Central

Americans fleeing wars devastating their countries (see chapter 6). "Undocumented" immigrant workers were showing up everywhere, not just in agriculture but also in the hotel-restaurant industry and subcontracted workshops for the automotive and other heavy industries.

In its June 23, 1980, issue, *Business Week* explained what was going on. It pointed out that because 7 million fewer young American workers were entering the labor force each decade, "the U.S. will need immigrants to buttress the labor supply if the economy is to grow." Once again America was being built by Latino labor. Counting "illegals," some 4 million Mexicans, 2.5 million Central Americans, and about half a million Dominicans came to the United States in the 1980s. Coincidentally, that adds up to the 7 million labor shortfall predicted by *Business Week*. Young people of Mexican descent were projected as second only to young whites as the largest source of new entrants into the labor force by the year 2000.[19]

Most economists realized that the new immigrants were helping to build the economy. As the business newspaper *The Wall Street Journal* reported on June 18, 1976, "Legal or not, the present wave of [illegal] Western Hemisphere immigrants may well be providing the margin of survival for entire sectors of the economy." The *Journal*'s May 7, 1985, headline added: "Illegal Immigrants Are Backbone of Economy in States of Southwest—They Make Computer Parts, Package Arthritis Pills, Cook, Clean and Baby-Sit—Prisoners in the Bunkhouse." The U.S. Forest Service used Mexican immigrants to reforest overcut or burned forests in a subcontracting system that was virtual slavery.[20]

The newly arriving Latinos were contributing to the economy in other ways too. A 1979 Labor Department study showed that over 75 percent of "undocumented workers" paid Social Security and income taxes, even though only 0.5 percent received welfare benefits and 1 percent used food stamps. The same workers' contributions accounted for a big chunk of the shrinking Social Security trust fund—as much as $80 billion a year. A 1984 Ford Foundation report confirmed that "as more whites reach Social Security age, their support will depend on Social Security taxes paid by an increasingly Hispanic and black workforce."[21]

Undocumented immigrants were working up to twelve hours a day for subminimum wages. They lived in terrible fear of being deported. "Yes, we would go out [for recreation] from time to time," one of them told an interviewer, "but we always lived tense with fear. Where the *migra* [Immigration and Naturalization Service or INS] usually grabbed us was at work."[22]

Some UFW and former UFW members realized that the "undocumented" Mexicans (and later the Central Americans) would have to be organized. *Their* rights would have to be addressed or else the UFW would be undermined the way the farmworkers' earlier unions had been.

In 1975, Orendain broke with Chavez and organized the independent Texas Farm Workers (TFW) to pay more attention to the "undocumented." In 1977, an organization with similar aims, the Arizona Farm Workers Union (AFWU), won the first labor contract ever to be signed by "undocumented" workers—the result of a hard-fought strike against Goldmar, Inc.'s Arrowhead Ranch, owned in part by Senator Barry Goldwater's brother. In 1980, the TFW, AFWU, and several other labor organizations in Mexico and the United States issued the Bill of Rights for Undocumented Workers (see chapter 6).

By the early 1980s, some 40,000 "undocumented" were unionized under the banner of the independent American Federation of Workers (AFW), founded by the TFWU, AFWU, and similar groups in Florida, California, Washington, and New York. It outnumbered Chavez's UFW two to one and included many service and industrial workers, especially in Los Angeles. It won so many strikes that it was able to persuade the AFL-CIO to instruct its affiliated

*The Texas Farm Workers union organized
undocumented workers who were farmworkers.*

unions to protect the "undocumented" against factory raids by *la migra*.[23]

The "new unionism" represented by groups like the AFW was showing up all over the country (see chapters 2 and 3). It aimed to achieve what earlier union movements had accomplished. To succeed, though, it realized it had to deal with the hard economic realities of "runaway shops" (companies that leave the country to take advantage of foreign cheap labor). Therefore, it often espoused transborder, *international* labor solidarity.

In the Southwest, Latino workers organized the Border Agricultural Workers Union that won a series of strikes on both sides of the U.S.-Mexico border. In the Midwest, a new union of mostly Mexican migrants from Texas, the Farm Labor Organizing Committee (FLOC), won a prolonged strike against the Campbell Soup Company but then faced possible defeat when Campbell threatened to move its Michigan operations to Sinaloa in northwestern Mexico. FLOC blocked the move by arranging for joint collective bargaining with its Sinaloan counterpart, the Mexican Farm Workers Union.[24]

As the "undocumented" organized, the mass media whipped up another "brown scare." President Jimmy Carter asked Congress to prohibit the hiring of "illegal aliens." Former CIA director William Colby claimed that Mexican immigration represented a greater future threat to the United States than did the Soviet Union. Conservative senator Alan Simpson called for making English the nation's "official language" and introduced the Simpson-Mazzoli bill, which eventually became the Immigration Reform and Control Law (IRCA, 1986).[25]

Meanwhile, Chavez's UFW launched another grape boycott in 1986 to alert the nation to new dangers: pesticides being sprayed on foods. A fifteen-minute UFW videotape entitled "Wrath of Grapes"[26] made its way into school classrooms. Millions of stunned youngsters learned about the seeping of pesticide sprays into underground sources

The farmworkers' union won a campaign to end spraying of grape vineyards with poisonous pesticides. UFW president Cesar Chavez speaks at a press conference about "contaminated" grapes.

of drinking water. They saw birth defects like missing limbs and deformed faces in young children of farmworkers and residents of communities near California's farm fields. Film narrator Mike Farrell informed them that "in town after town in California's Central Valley children are being stricken with cancer." A photograph of a hulky white McFarland football player who died of cancer appeared.

In the middle of the video, youngsters watched and listened in disbelief as a housewife held a tasty-looking bunch of grapes under the kitchen faucet and Farrell told them:

> *One third of the pesticides used on grapes are known to cause cancer. The California Department of Agriculture found residues of captan and ten other pesticides on grapes they sampled. Most of these residues cannot be completely washed off. The long-term effects of pesticides on consumers are unknown and may not show up for many years. In 1984 California's growers used more than 300 million tons of pesticides, some of the most toxic chemicals ever manufactured.*

The film went on to tell how California's governor vetoed a bill requiring growers to post signs warning about pesticides because "California's 14 billion dollar a year agribusiness couldn't afford the signs."

The "Wrath of Grapes" video begins with the shot of an airplane spraying a grape field and Chavez's voice saying, "We are declaring war, war on the pesticides that are poisoning and killing our people." It ends with the shots of victims and Chavez explaining: "We need to meet the growers and stop their madness at the marketplace. If enough people join us and don't buy grapes, the growers will have to do something about the pesticides, at least in grapes, and once we get grapes we can go and get other products too."

Chavez died in 1993 at age sixty-six, his work unfinished. But as youngsters who saw the film told their parents about it, the grape boycott and war against dangerous pesticides gained momentum. Under increasing pressure from environmentalists influenced by the farmworkers, the federal government banned the use of at least a few of the more suspect pesticides.

Once again, as people sat down at their magnificently stocked holiday tables—their foods hopefully safer than before—only a few were aware of the Latinos who had sacrificed so much to build a well-fed, environmentally safe, and healthy America. Even fewer thought about the tremendous contribution Latinos make to our health care system.

2 *dos*

THE HEALTH CARE

PROVIDERS

The first principle of medical ethics is to offer compassion and respect for human dignity. For me, this pledge includes the illegal alien dying of AIDS.

—Mexican-American doctor
Aliza Lifshitz, 1992[1]

When they worry about their health, most Americans visualize doctors—usually white. They don't think about the dozens of other indispensable health care workers, frequently Latinos and African Americans. Doctors do. They realize that without these workers, they can't even begin to do their jobs.

Imagine a serious accident or disaster. Emergency medical technicians jump into an ambulance and rush to the scene. Doctors, nurses, nurses' aides, physician assistants, medical assistants, and orderlies in area hospitals rush about preparing for the arrival of injured people. At their computers and filing cabinets, medical records clerks locate files to assist both staff and patients. Pharmacists and their assistants in the hospital dispensary assemble extra bandages, antibiotics, and other supplies so there will be enough on hand to handle the emergency.

As the injured people arrive, other health care professionals swing into action. Laboratory technicians and medical technologists perform X rays, sonograms, and CAT scans on complex machines in order to locate hard-to-spot internal injuries. In operating rooms, anesthesiologists, surgical nurses, and technologists help the surgeons save lives.

In the days that follow, dietitians, nutritionists, cooks, and kitchen workers make sure that patients eat the right foods. Armies of nurses and nurses' aides carry out the doctors' orders, changing burn dressings, administering injections sent up by the pharmacist, and keeping the patients clean and as comfortable as possible. Later, physical therapists help the victims recover the use of injured muscles and limbs. Social workers, psychotherapists, and other mental health workers counsel the emotionally upset patients and their distraught families. Maintenance personnel and orderlies bustle about mopping, sweeping, hauling oxygen equipment, repairing air conditioners, and keeping every part of the hospital sanitary and in working order.

That's how it's supposed to work. But by the 1990s,

increasing numbers of Americans were complaining about a deteriorating health care system charging outlandish fees, and a new president said the system was "broken." For most Latinos and other people not so well off, the situation has become critical. They are the bulk of the more than a quarter of the nation's people who have no health care insurance. They are forced to postpone preventive measures like physical checkups and regular medical care during pregnancies and chronic illnesses, as well as immunizations for their children. They cannot afford the high fees of private doctors or take time out from work to sit for hours in overcrowded public clinics waiting for a handful of overworked doctors to examine them. So they often have to ignore symptoms and hope they will get well on their own. Add to this poor diets and substandard housing conditions, and the problems are multiplied.

The hospitals in inner city slum neighborhoods compare unfavorably to our "ideal" hospital scenario at the start of this chapter. Private hospitals are financed by better-off patients covered by health insurance. They also receive handsome contributions from wealthy donors. The hospitals compete for patients by improving their services. Overcrowded public hospitals in poor areas are barely kept afloat by near-bankrupt cities. To make the dollars stretch, all services are reduced. The latest expensive equipment is usually absent or broken.

On July 8, 1993, a headline in the *New York Times*— "Big Health Gap Tied to Income"—didn't surprise many people. The *Times* news story documented the widening gap in health care services for rich and poor and singled out the extra burdens put on the shoulders of nonwhites. Not only are the poor receiving substandard or nonexistent health care, but they are *dying* from illnesses far more often, with the difference in mortality rates *more than doubling* in twenty-five years.

The *Times'* "Big Health Gap" story reflects the immense income differences dividing the nation into an increasingly two-tiered society dominated by a relatively small number of well-off, mostly white people. Even at the very low level of income set by the government to define the word "poor," the numbers of people below this "poverty line" are growing and the racial gaps are widening. U.S. Census data show only a tenth of whites are "poor," compared with 40.6 percent of Puerto Ricans, 31.9 percent of African Americans, and 28.1 percent of all Latinos.[2]

Some people, especially Latinos and African Americans, have long fought against the obstacles to a decent health care system. They have won several major victories. An early one rectified an especially dangerous and racist situation. Most people go to the nearest hospital when they are suddenly injured or gravely ill. For poor people, this means an inferior "city" hospital. If they can, they dash to the emergency rooms of the better hospitals in more prosperous middle-class neighborhoods. Decades ago, when some injured or ailing children died after middle-class hospitals turned them away because of inability to pay, early Latino and African-American reformers and a few white supporters publicized the shameful situation widely. As a result of their campaign, federally funded programs like Medicaid were introduced that guaranteed government payment of medical bills for the poor. New laws were also passed prohibiting hospitals from refusing service. If a baby in a slum apartment were bitten by a rat or another family member awakened in the night with a raging fever, *any* hospital emergency room had to provide treatment.

Another problem deeply affecting the health status of Latinos remains unsolved. There is a severe shortage of Latino physicians and nurses. By 1985, despite the passage of laws prohibiting discrimination, almost all the nation's doctors and nurses were white. Of more than half a million physicians, only 17,600 were Latino, a mere 3.4 percent (3 percent were African American). Latinos accounted for even fewer nurses: 1.6 percent of the 1.5 million Registered Nurses (4.5 percent African American). Of the country's half million licensed "practical nurses," Latinos were 2.5 percent (African Americans 14.9). The situation was no better in dentistry and pharmacology. In 1987 there were *only 109* Latino graduates from the nation's twenty-four schools of public health enrolling 8,500 students.[3]

At a 1985 conference of medical school deans and presidents, participants discussed the importance of increasing the number of Latino and African-American doctors and nurses. They noted that few white health practitioners attend to nonwhite clientele. Moreover, they discussed the tendency among white male physicians to take the complaints of nonwhites and females less seriously. Some made a connection between the health problems of Latinos and African Americans and the shortage of minority physicians.

To answer arguments that trained minority physicians might stay away from poor neighborhoods too, they cited the fact that up to 80 percent of minority health professions graduates "practice in or adjacent to health manpower shortage areas that have overwhelmingly minority populations where health services are most needed." One conference participant stated:

> *I can tell you from my own experience there is real happiness and gratification from providing good health care to minority persons where you are really needed, where your presence makes a difference and where you can talk and act naturally. Your patients really appreciate you and relate to you very well. It is a very positive, gratifying experience.*[4]

The urgent need for Latino skilled medical personnel became especially obvious after a horrible shooting incident known as the McDonald's Massacre in 1984. A psychologically disturbed white unemployed security guard, right after calling the local health center asking for immediate help and not getting it, went to a McDonald's restaurant in the border community of San Ysidro, California. The town of 13,500 is about 90 percent Mexican and Mexican American. The heavily armed man opened fire on everyone and, after forty minutes of mayhem, was finally himself gunned down by police. By the time ambulances arrived twenty-one lay dead, fifteen injured.

At the health center and nearby hospitals, the wounded, some of them Mexicans who spoke no English, faced long delays and abrupt, even rude treatment at the hands of doctors and nurses who spoke little or no Spanish. The most sympathy and understanding for the terrified victims came from the most overlooked hospital employees—floor sweepers, kitchen help, orderlies, and practical nurses and nurses' aides who took temperatures or changed the sheets. Many of them "just happened to be" Latino!

Afterward, a great number of people were in serious need of psychological help. There were not enough trained psychotherapists. Only a few of the persons suffering from Post-Traumatic Stress Disorder (PTSD) received the attention of a doctor. Fortunately, support of the town's residents for all the victims and their families was very strong.[5]

Because of the inferior reputation of so many city hospitals and the lack of Latino doctors and nurses, some Latinos rely on barrio healers called *curanderas* and *curanderos*—female and male healers. *Curanderas* called *parteras*, or midwives, attend to pregnant women. Spiritualism also plays a role among some Latinos, especially in the mental health care of Puerto Ricans.

In Colonial America, similar Euroamerican healers called midwives, domestic practitioners, and "kitchen physics" also delivered babies and ministered to the sick. Physicians were not highly regarded. Financially well-off patients often refused the doctor's services and turned instead to the respected "domestic practitioners." Prior to the late 1800s, most doctors used harsh methods to treat their patients. Leeches, enemas, and laxatives were their main weapons against illness. Native American and

Mexican-American medicine men and women thought that the medical practices of the white men were useless. They preferred gentle herbal preparations, cleanliness, and loving care of the sick. Yankee domestic practitioners agreed with them. Recent historical research has shown that the women treated by midwives—white, Latina, and so-called "Black grannies" in the South—were better off than those cared for by the increasingly powerful white male medical establishment.[6]

Modern American medicine owes much to these earlier healers. From the first days of the "discovery" of Latin America, Europeans were greatly impressed by how swiftly and well the Indians cured illnesses and war wounds. They began collecting herbal medicines and interviewing *curanderas* and *curanderos* to learn of the curative properties of a tremendous variety of medicinal plants they had never seen before. Important contributions to modern medicine resulted, including the discovery of many drugs like fever-reducing quinine.

Because they recognize the importance of these natural sources for pharmaceutical products, medical researchers are among the first to call for laws protecting Latin America's disappearing tropical rain forests. These lush areas contain millions of yet unresearched plant specimens that might contribute to the treatment of cancer and other diseases. Scientists, along with pharmaceutical companies, are also worried about the possible extinction of rain forest Indians, because some of the "natives" possess key secrets to medicinal plant science.[7]

A dwindling number of Latinos still rely on *curanderas* and *parteras*, particularly in remote rural areas or in some of the urban slums. These Latinos appreciate a *curandera*'s low fees and warm caring approach in the Spanish language, often accompanied by familiar religious symbols or prayers.

But most Latinos feel they deserve all of the benefits of the new medical technologies that save the lives of others.

Many have chosen careers in medicine in order to help their suffering people. Unable to afford the tremendous expense of medical schools and nursing schools, they have taken jobs in the lower echelons of health care. They are the unsung, underpaid heroines and heroes of hospitals and clinics all over the nation.

There are 4 million of these so-called "allied health professionals." Three-quarters of them are women. African Americans and Latinas fill the lowest-paid categories of this workforce, their salaries often falling below the poverty line.

A new term has been invented to describe this growing phalanx of underpaid workers in America: the "working poor." They appear in all kinds of economic activities, from manufacturing sweatshops and small businesses to clerking and washing dishes. Their lack of economic resources—and for many the color of their skin—explains why the working poor are unable to become doctors or nurses in the first place. As one researcher of the health care field has pointed out: "They do not have the money or encouragement for further training so they become the aides, hospital cooks, attendants, practical nurses and office clerks."[8]

Recognizing the overlooked importance of lower-echelon health workers in providing good health care, a number of Latino and African-American activists began organizing labor unions of these "working poor" to upgrade their salary and work conditions. The oldest and most famous of them is New York City's independent 100,000-member District 1199 of the national Drug, Hospital and Health Care Employees Union, which won its first victory among hospital employees at a Bronx hospital in 1958. It is currently led by Dennis Rivera, a college dropout from Puerto Rico, former nursing home janitor, and influential pro-labor voice in the Democratic Party.

Rivera became 1199's president in 1989 after helping to lead a successful "save the union" campaign against those wanting to limit the newfound power of the expanding membership. Noting that the nation's giant labor-union

Dennis Rivera, president of Local 1199 of the
hospital workers' union (right), and Jesse Jackson

conglomerate AFL-CIO often "has more in common with
the employers than with the rank and file," Rivera has accel-
erated 1199's unionization of the lowest-paid and fastest-
growing layers of health care employees—mostly African-

American and Latina women who work in nursing homes, outpatient facilities, home health care organizations, and independent clinics.[9]

Increasing the numbers of African-American and Latino doctors and nurses is an even more difficult challenge. It costs a person far less to train for the "allied health professions" where jobs are readily available. "Without financial support" for minorities, the 1985 conference of deans report emphasized, "motivation, recruitment and strong academic programs will go for naught."[10]

Before the civil rights movement won laws guaranteeing more equal opportunities for nonwhite minorities in the mid-1960s, *and special government scholarships and loans to finance college studies,* one hardly *ever* saw a Latino doctor or nurse (and very few white woman doctors either). After those victories, for the first time, Latinos, Native Americans, African Americans, and women started to make some significant inroads into the medical profession. Even so, in the heavily Latino state of Texas, the University of Texas medical school did not graduate a single Latina woman until 1969. And not until 1989 did a Latino achieve national office in the health care field. That year, Puerto Rican pediatrician Dr. Antonia Novello became the first woman and first nonwhite to assume the post of surgeon general of the United States. With economic hard times starting in the mid-1970s and continuing into the 1990s, the rate of increase for nonwhite enrollees and graduates in medical and nursing schools started leveling off in the mid-1970s, cutting the gains.[11]

Why are Latinos still so underrepresented in the higher echelons of the health care professions? The most often noted reasons are racial discrimination in the educational system; the rising costs of attending medical schools; and the decline in available scholarships. At the deans' conference, Eastern Virginia Medical School Dean Richard G. Lester commented on a "lack of understanding" among most whites of the fact that even "educated, professional" non-

Dr. Antonia Novello, Puerto Rican
pediatrician and first woman and first nonwhite
to assume the post of U.S. surgeon general

whites "still live on the edge and are not part of society as a whole." Like others, Dean Lester recommended not only changes in white professionals' attitudes but "changing the total educational system."[12]

Even to have an outside chance to apply to a nursing or medical school, a Latino or African American must first get a good education in grade school and high school. Since school budgets come largely from the taxes paid by local residents, ghetto schools are, like ghetto hospitals, inferior to the schools in other neighborhoods. The conference report of the medical school deans and presidents summed the matter up this way: "[Because of] the brutal reality of money, a major barrier for minority students is a substandard general education, from an early age, culminating in poor quality science teaching in some high schools and even in some colleges."[13]

As we shall see in chapter 4, generations of Latinos and African Americans have worked to improve the schools their children attend. Again, money to finance the needed changes has not been provided.

At their 1985 conference, the medical school leaders recommended the goals of "a 15 percent minority student admissions rate by 1990" *and* implementation of measures to recruit, retain, and graduate them. However, the state of public school education makes it obvious why the goals are not being reached.

Many Latinos realize that without people organizing to insist upon implementation of even the conference's relatively inexpensive recommendations, statistics and conference reports are easily forgotten or filed away. They know that their greatest victories have come when they have mobilized giant demonstrations in the streets, as happened in the 1960s.

In those earlier times, Latinos, like other Americans, joined the many social movements demanding a more decent country. In the Latino barrios of the South Bronx a coalition of patients and health workers took over Lincoln

Hospital in 1970. They set up a day care center in one of the rundown hospital's unused buildings and called for better facilities and services. Sponsors of the takeover included the Young Lords, a group of Puerto Rican young women and men, some of them former gang members. The Young Lords set up "people's health clinics" and "breakfast-for-children" programs all around New York and other cities.

Puerto Rican Dr. Helen Rodriguez, director of Lincoln's Department of Pediatrics from 1970 to 1974, later recalled her feelings about the hospital takeover: "I felt I had literally crossed a bridge. I could never lead the quiet, respectable life of an academic again, nor did I want to."[14] It was one of the early harbingers of what grew into a widespread community-oriented health care movement aimed at overcoming the nation's dual-track health care system—one for the rich, one for the poor.

In the late 1970s, South Bronx residents, allied with concerned feminist and health activists from the rest of New York, demanded additional improvements at Lincoln, including more Spanish-speaking directors and doctors like Rodriguez. They won most of their demands. But even then, they were shocked and hurt when they learned that the newly appointed male Spanish-speaking head of obstetrics-gynecology had served earlier in Puerto Rico's population control program that sterilized more than one-third of Puerto Rico's women of reproductive age.[15]

Meanwhile, as health problems have grown worse for almost all Americans, hospitals in predominantly Latino and African-American neighborhoods have been unable to meet the demands of community-oriented movements for improved care and labor conditions. The hospitals are plagued by overcrowding, understaffing, and declining cure rates. Every now and then the shockingly unhealthy conditions and scandals in inner city hospitals are discussed on local evening television news broadcasts. City officials and hospital administrators then step before the cameras to reassure us the situation will be corrected. But little is done, and the *Times*' "Big Health Gap Tied to Income" widens. The spread of AIDS/HIV is affecting a disproportionate number of Latinos, especially Puerto Ricans.

Many Americans voted Bill Clinton into the presidency in 1992 precisely because he promised to do something about the deteriorating health care situation. A few months after he took office, he announced a new health plan. In late 1993, he sent a letter to millions of Americans. "For the first time in our nation's history," he promised, "we can guarantee that virtually no American family will fall through the cracks in America's health care system."

Latinos learned that immigrants without "legal papers" would be allowed to "fall through the cracks." Consequently, an estimated number of up to 5 million people would be excluded from coverage. Since viruses do not recognize people's citizenship, advocates for the human rights of the much abused immigrants noted that their exclusion was illogical, unhealthy, and potentially very costly. It also was a case of "taxation without representation," they said. "Illegal" immigrant workers would continue to have taxes deducted from their paychecks yet be denied services funded by the taxes.[16]

At the outset of this chapter, Mexican-American doctor Aliza Lifshitz, president of the 1,300-member California Hispanic American Medical Association, points to the immorality of denying *anyone* health care. It remains to be seen if millions of Americans will demand that her pledge be fulfilled.

3 *tres*

Building
a Decent
Work
Life

*[The world-famous copper mining area of
Arizona was] built entirely by Mexican labor
. . . cheaply . . . and admirably.*
> —Mining millionaire James Colquhoun,
> *The Early History of the Clifton-Morenci
> District,* 1924

*America is so rich and fat, because it has eaten
the tragedy of millions of immigrants.*
> —Journalist Michael Gold, *Jews Without
> Money,* 1930

Work is a central part of all of our lives. Our most productive, wide-awake hours are spent away from home, working. If our jobs are interesting, pay decent wages, and include vacations, health care, and an old-age pension, we feel lucky. We can then enjoy leisure time for sports, travel, hobbies with friends and family. We can eat well, take advantage of the latest in medical knowledge, and afford improved education for our children.

Nations whose citizens have a high standard of living are admired and envied throughout the world by nations of starving, slaving people. Providing decent jobs for everyone is central to building a better America. Even before the Civil War, working people began to realize that isolated and alone, they could make few changes to improve their lives. Labor unions, much maligned in recent times, became central to the battle for better work conditions and wages.

"Battle" is the right word for the century-long fight for decent wages and work conditions. When the United States first began industrializing, people earned as little as 15 cents for sixteen-hour days.[1] In Lowell, Massachusetts, site of the first textile factories, eleven-year-old girls were housed in prisonlike dormitories. Their workplaces were filled with the noise of machinery. The air they breathed was laden with minute particles of lint from the heavy rolls of cloth, inflaming their lungs. Many of them died young of "white lung," caused by years of breathing the polluted air.

The bravest workers became labor organizers, trying to form unions. They frequently faced bullets or jailings for the supposed crime of demanding the basic human rights we take for granted today—the eight-hour work day, minimum wage, unemployment insurance, Social Security, a ban on child labor. It took nearly half a century to win even these minimal demands.

For workers, going on strike usually meant weeks and even months without a paycheck. The factory owners could hold out. Although they resented losing profits during strikes, their dinner tables remained piled high with food. They recruited "scabs" (strikebreaking employees), often hungry and desperate unemployed people, to take the place of the strikers. The factory heads hired labor spies to join the unions and keep them informed of developments. Armed goon squads were well paid to beat up pro-union workers, and frequently friends of the owners in high government posts sent in state militia and federal troops to break strikes.

The wealthiest employers were predominantly white Anglo-Saxon Protestants. They encouraged a racial-ethnic-religious pecking order, with African Americans placed at the bottom. Next came Chinese, other Asians, and darker-skinned Latinos. U.S.-born white workers were treated better than new immigrants. Protestants were treated better than Catholics and Jews. Racial and linguistic differences were used to divide workers against one another. The words of a popular American folk song summed it up: "If you're white, you're right; if you're brown, stick roun'; but if you're black, get back!" Railroad baron Jay Gould boasted: "I can hire one half of the working class to kill the other half."[2]

In the Southwest, where more than 100,000 Mexicans became U.S. citizens after Mexico lost nearly half its territory in the U.S.-Mexico War (1846–1848), invading white settlers drove the Mexicans from their lands, mines, and homes in order to "settle the frontier." Mexicans were frequently lynched in those early times. The whites were backed up by federal troops and local lawmen like the Texas Rangers—*los rinches*. Many Mexicans lost their possessions even before the 1846 war, especially in Texas and California.

But the whites still welcomed cheap Mexican labor to do the hardest work. Low-paid labor was needed urgently to replace the Chinese "coolies," as they were called, who were expelled in 1882. Congress had responded to the pressures of a nationwide labor movement by passing new laws against contract labor. Exempted from the new laws, however, were "foreigners temporarily residing in the U.S."—a loophole permitting the contracting of Mexicans to work in the mines, rail yards, and farm fields.

Over the next several decades, as labor recruiters fanned out, more than 1.7 million Mexicans moved to the United States—one of the largest movements of a people in recorded history. By 1940, there were about 2.5 million Mexicans in the United States, most of them U.S. citizens by then. A report issued by the U.S. commissioner general of immigration in 1910 explained the Mexicans' great migration: "The principal reason underlying this increase is the extensive industrial development now taking place."[3]

Millions of southern and eastern European immigrants also arrived to help build the nation into an industrial colossus. Most of the immigrants lived hard lives. Mexicans fared even worse because of their darker skin color and the poisonous legacy of the 1846 war.

In the Southwest, Mexicans received 50 cents a day for cutting, hauling, and laying railway ties. In the mines, they had to work at least two hours more per day than other workers and at half the pay. Their paychecks were slips of paper redeemable at the company store stocked with high-priced clothing and food. Mine owner Sylvester Mowry boasted that he paid "his" Mexicans one dollar a day "in large part in merchandise at large profits."[4]

Because of their fear of being shipped back across the border, Mexicans worked harder than most others. Very few Mexicans were promoted to better jobs, even though they were some of the most talented workers the West ever knew. As an American mechanic observed in 1908:

They will never pay a Mexican what he's really worth compared with a white man. I know a Mexican that's the best blacksmith I ever knew. He has made some of the best tools I ever used. But they pay him $1.50 a day as a helper, working under an American blacksmith who gets 7 dollars a day.[5]

When other workers asked for higher wages, they were warned by the mine owners that they could always be replaced by lower-paid Mexicans. Not only were Mexican miners forced to live on starvation wages, but they were frequently attacked, even lynched, by angry Anglo and immigrant workers blaming them for their own inadequate wages. A noted historian wrote in 1889 that white people carried out frequent "acts of lawless violence, including murders, robberies, and lynching . . . of the hated 'greasers.'"[6]

The Mexicans were segregated into wretched shacks in the worst parts of the mining towns—on hillsides subject to erosion and sudden landslides or at low points regularly swept by devastating flash floods. Other townspeople nicknamed the barrios "jimtown," "frogtown," or "Greaserville."

In the world's richest copper area, the mining triangle linking the U.S.-owned mines of northern Sonora (Mexico) to those of southern Arizona and a corner of New Mexico, most of the mine workers were Mexican. The main Arizona deposits were discovered in the 1870s—oxidized ores with up to 55 percent copper layered beneath the earth to depths of 2,200 feet! After Mexicans developed some of the first copper and gold mine sites in New Mexico, Arizona, and California, they taught newly arriving "Anglo" prospectors and investors their techniques. At first appreciated for their skills, the Mexicans were soon victimized.

During the 1849 gold rush, tens of thousands of gold-hungry "forty-niners" swarmed over northern California's mining areas, attacking any "foreigners," as the Latinos were called, who got in their way. One state congressman compared Latinos to "the beast in the field . . . a curse to any enlightened community."[7] Liquored-up mobs attacked Mexican, Chilean, and Peruvian miners, raped Latina women, and went on lynching sprees against the very men who had taught them how to pan the gold. The violence, high taxes placed on "foreign" miners, and new discriminatory land-title laws drove Latinos out of the area. Outnumbered ten to one, most Mexican "Californianos"

Prospecting for gold during the California Gold Rush

moved south to the Los Angeles area. In Los Angeles the Spanish-language newspaper *El Clamor Público* (Public Outcry) quipped that Euroamerican democracy looked more like *Linchocracia*.[8]

In the rest of the Southwest, Mexicans fared no better. With the exception of some of the elites (*ricos*) who formed alliances or intermarried with their Anglo counterparts, Mexicans lost their properties and became underpaid workers. Their fathers and grandfathers had taught the invading Anglos new skills, everything from dry-process mining for extracting silver, copper, and quartz to irrigation techniques passed down for generations from the Spanish and Indians. One copper company executive was honest enough to praise the Mexicans' skills in mining and smelting, noting that the huge Arizona copper bonanza was "built entirely by Mexican labor . . . cheaply . . . and admirably."[9]

In Arizona, once Mexicans got the copper and other mines and smelters going, absentee owners of the Longfellow Copper Company, Phelps Dodge, and other corporations returned to oversee the production of hundreds of thousands of tons of ore dug out by the Mexicans and other workers. By 1916 the United States was producing 63 percent of the world's copper. Arizona accounted for half of it. Without that copper, the electrical industry would not have been able to generate the huge quantities of power needed to industrialize America (see Introduction).

Copper mining was hard and dangerous work. Few native-born Americans wanted any part of it. Using explosives, picks, and shovels, the Mexicans sank the shafts to get at the mining triangle's rich ores. They then drove "drifts" along the ore veins, and hacked out openings called "raises" to connect the various levels. Occasionally, they extended the raises to the surface to provide ventilation or emergency escape routes. They next blasted and hacked out the ore piece by piece along the veins and shoveled it into chutes and train cars for transport to the shafts, where it was dumped into "pockets," drawn into "skips," and hoisted up the shafts to the surface. Aboveground, trains waited to haul the valuable ore to smelters and refineries, many of them thousands of miles back East, where copper from South America was also being processed.

At times the miners could hardly breathe, so thick was the air with bits of rock and dirt. Cave-ins came without warning. Within seconds dozens of men would be buried alive, cut off from any exit, suffocating. Hardly a miner lived who did not know of one friend or relative killed or crippled in an accident.[10]

Spending most of their lives in the cold, wet, dark caverns of the mines, breathing air fouled by mineral dust, miners contracted lung diseases. When they could no longer work, they had no workmen's compensation. They relied on the charity of their fellow workers. Doctors were seldom seen in copper country, where there were no fat fees waiting. Miners in the greater Clifton area in the early 1900s were profoundly grateful for the services of Teresa Urrea, a world-famous *curandera* from Cabora, Mexico. She tended to their needs so well that some called her the "Saint of Cabora." With monies she gained from a national speaking tour arranged by wealthy bankers, Teresa built a hospital in Clifton, shortly before she died of tuberculosis in 1906 at the age of thirty-three.[11]

Not only in the mines but in many other places where new industries sprang up and railroads were built, Mexicans played an indispensable role in turning the United States into an economic powerhouse. The railroad yards, slaughterhouses, and meat-packing plants of Kansas City, Chicago, and Milwaukee echoed with the Spanish accents heard in Mexico's northern and central cities of Hermosillo, Torreón, and San Luis Potosí.

Before and after the Civil War, Latinos fought for decent work conditions for everyone. Out West, the word "huelga" was heard before its English equivalent "strike." In Florida, where Cuban exiles and refugees from the Thirty Years War against Spain (1868–1898) built up the cigar

Inside a mine in Colorado

Mexicans working on a railroad

industry, Cuban tobacco union leaders supported the country's first big national labor organization, the Knights of Labor, founded in 1869. The Knights initially accepted Latinos, who welcomed the chance to join with other Americans to attempt to make life for working people worth living. Mexicans were among the first to walk out during the gigantic 1877 national rail strike that was crushed by federal troops at the cost of a hundred lives. In 1885, refusing to knuckle under to the railroad millionaires, Mexicans helped win a strike that threatened Jay Gould's southwest railroads. Their victory lent momentum to a nationwide strike movement demanding the eight-hour day in several industries. The following year, 1886, was called "the year of the great uprising of labor," as half a million workers conducted 1,400 strikes.[12]

Over the next decades it seemed almost everyone was talking "union" and "eight hours." In the 1890s, the eight-hour-day movement hit full stride. People rallied to new radical leaders like the popular socialist Eugene Debs, who was later to run for the presidency and draw a million votes. The nation erupted in strikes, the most famous being the Homestead strike in Pennsylvania against Carnegie Steel and the American Railway Union's strike against Pullman.

Successful strikes created a fragile unity among all workers. But when times were hard or strikes were lost, Mexicans frequently were blamed irrationally for the problems. During a severe depression in 1893, violence against Mexicans increased, and the unions expelled them. Despite this abuse by their fellow workers, the Mexicans, alone again in their mutual-aid types of unions known as *mutualistas*, continued to express their desire to unite with other workers.

In Arizona, a hard-won unity between Mexicans and European immigrants made a big difference. After the passage of a state law mandating an eight-hour day, Mexicans were told they still had to work ten hours or more because the law excluded foreigners. In 1903 the *mutualistas* in the valuable Morenci-Metcalf-Clifton copper mines struck again. Some 1,600 workers, including Slavs and other European immigrants, also excluded from the eight-hour legislation, walked off the job. The press called it "the Mexican affair." The workers demanded the eight-hour-day, protection against unjust firings, fair prices at the company stores, free medical care when they were injured at work, paid life insurance, and an end to the hiring of nonunion and non-*mutualista* members. In the midst of the strike, a flash flood swept away miners' shacks and killed fifty people. While the miners grieved for their dead, they maintained the strike. Finally Arizona Rangers, federal troops, and national guardsmen—the biggest show of force since the Indian wars—crushed it.[13]

But the struggle did not end there. To give up meant to go on with an unbearably difficult life, working until you dropped or were killed in the mine, and hearing your children cry from hunger at night. The 1903 copper strike was only the beginning of labor actions sparked by discontented Mexican workers and some of the millions of newly arriving European immigrants toiling to industrialize America. After the copper strike, the Western Federation of Miners (WFM) began admitting Mexicans. In 1905 it helped organize the IWW, better known as the Wobblies.

Calling for "one big union" of all workers, the Wobblies' men and women leaders advocated a government run by working people, a true "industrial democracy." Mexicans liked the sound of that. One of their own, Lucía González, a famed labor organizer and orator since the 1880s, attended the IWW's founding convention. Lucy, as she was known, advocated equal pay for equal work, whatever a person's race or gender. Another famed woman union organizer, Mary Harris Jones, whom mine and rail workers called Mother Jones, also attended. Within a decade Mexicans and Mexican Americans accounted for half of the IWW's dues.[14]

Most working people knew that union organizers and

others who dared to help them were singled out by the owners of the mines and mills. Ricardo Flores Magón, Abraham Salcido, and several other men and women of the Mexican Liberal Party (PLM) were attempting a revolution against Mexico's oppressive dictatorship. Many of the miners knew Salcido well. He and other PLM militants had been jailed for leading the 1903 Arizona copper strike and a similar strike in Cananea, Sonora, in 1906. When Flores Magón and other PLM leaders were arrested by U.S. authorities, the Wobblies called for a national movement to free the Mexican political prisoners. Many Mexicans joined with other trade unionists and several prominent politicians and writers in a successful campaign for their release. Not willing to keep quiet, PLM leaders were arrested time and time again.

As more and more of the nation's immigrants organized and feelings of solidarity among working people spread, it was more difficult for employers to find willing scabs as strikebreakers were called. A few strikes concluded in victories for the workers, but the majority ended in violent defeat. The eight-hour day was a long way off, and child labor remained widespread, especially in agriculture.

Journalist Upton Sinclair's widely read novel *The Jungle* (1906) shocked many Americans with its descriptions of the unsafe and unsanitary conditions at the stockyards and meat-packing houses where many Mexicans worked. Newspapers ran exposé articles about similarly dangerous conditions in other industries. As a result of the publicity and the labor movement's constant pressures, a few worker safety and health laws were legislated—an historic first.

But employers frequently ignored the new rules. In 1911, the Triangle Shirtwaist Company fire in New York City killed 146 people, most of them young Italian and Jewish seamstresses. At Triangle, the bosses had blocked many fire exits to create wall space for extra sewing machines. Other doors were kept locked so that foremen could keep a closer eye on their employees. There were no fire escapes, and fire truck ladders could not reach the high floors. Screaming women and men jumped from tenth-floor windows, their clothes ablaze. Newspaper readers all over the nation were shocked, and more people started to sympathize with the union movement.

During that period, the 2-million strong AFL decided to accept the Mexican immigrants' Unión de Jornaleros Unidos [United Dayworkers Union] of California as an affiliate. Traditionally, the AFL had turned away Mexicans, viewing them as potential strikebreakers. AFL leader Samuel Gompers publicly referred to Mexicans' "inferior capacity to produce" and described them as a "menace" and a "great evil."[15] But Mexicans who were imported to break strikes soon realized they had been tricked and became pro-union.

Conditions at the nation's mines remained intolerably bad. Mexicans and Europeans continued to lead strikes demanding improvements. A prolonged coal-mining strike by thousands of Mexican, Greek, Serb, and Italian members of the United Mine Workers (UMW) in southern Colorado led to the dreadful Ludlow Massacre. In 1913–1914, evicted from company housing, the striking miners and their families set up tent colonies. Company owners called in the militia, who one morning machine-gunned the main settlement in Ludlow. At dusk, National Guardsmen set the tents on fire. People ran for cover, their clothes in flames. Twenty-six people, including at least eleven Mexicans, died; eight were children. The miners fought back but were outgunned by federal troops. In all, sixty-six died before the strike ended.[16] When they heard about it, people across the nation protested the shocking Ludlow Massacre. Under public pressure, a presidential commission was appointed to investigate. Its report revealed the obvious: the incinerated miners were murdered and the company bosses were at fault. No punitive measures were ever taken. The most important boss, millionaire John D. Rockefeller, never even

*An IWW parade in New York City to support
the striking miners of Ludlow, Colorado*

bothered to apologize, although he eventually allowed company-controlled unions in the Colorado mines as a "concession."

The Triangle and Ludlow events, rather than discourage workers, increased their determination to win the right to at least a bearable life. The choices were obvious. Fighting back was risky, but nothing would ever change unless the workers organized. In 1915, three Mexican mine unions carried out a four-month strike in the Clifton area's copper mines to insist on a $3.50-per-day minimum for *all* underground miners regardless of race. Despite the presence of the National Guard, the thousands of strikers won their main demands. Five thousand unionized Mexican miners then united with other workers to launch a massive two-year strike wave against the big copper companies to gain better conditions. President Woodrow Wilson dispatched 100,000 federalized National Guardsmen to help put down the crippling strike wave.

The press fanned flames of anti-Mexican hysteria into roaring fires. Mexicans were scapegoated for the 1913 economic depression, the growing labor unrest, and the border turbulence swirling around the Mexican Revolution of 1910–1917. After the Mexican revolutionary leader Pancho Villa's 1916 raid on Columbus, New Mexico—in retaliation for President Wilson's ban on arms shipments across the border and diplomatic recognition of Villa's more conservative rival—it became open season on Mexicans.[17]

In Europe, thousands of young French, English, and Russian men were losing their lives in the trench warfare of World War I, which had been raging for three long years (1914–1917). Just one month before the United States entered the conflict in April 1917, the U.S. Congress passed the Jones Act making Puerto Ricans U.S. citizens. Puerto Rico had become a U.S. colony in 1898 when American soldiers occupied several islands of the declining Spanish empire, including Cuba, where guerrilla fighters had already brought Spain to her knees. The congressmen realized that as citizens, young Puerto Rican men could be drafted into the army.[18]

Eighteen thousand young Puerto Ricans were mobilized and sent off to fight in segregated units. The Jones Act permitted them to die for the United States, but it did not allow them to vote in presidential elections, a rule that still leaves Puerto Ricans second-class citizens today. Their representation in the U.S. Congress was limited to a voteless resident commissioner in the House of Representatives. As a concession, residents (and businesses) on the island were exempted from U.S. taxes. This did not help the poor much, since most of them didn't earn enough to be taxed, but it was a windfall for U.S. corporations. The first of the runaway plants, so common in the 1980s, made a beeline for tax-free Puerto Rico.

During the war, employers waved the banner of patriotism in an attempt to roll back the gains of the labor movement. Anyone striving for better wages or conditions was labeled a traitor or even a German spy. On the one hand, Mexicans were accused of being pro-German subversives. On the other hand, the government further expanded legal importation of contracted Mexican workers in 1917 because of labor shortages caused by American workers going off to Europe to fight.

Feverish with racism and "patriotism," nativist (hostile to foreigners) groups attacked Mexicans, determined to rid the country of "aliens." Encouraged by employers attempting to dampen the spirit of the union movement, the mobs especially singled out union activists. In June 1917, a vicious act took place in Bisbee, Arizona, where miners had recently joined the strike wave. Racist members of the Bisbee Loyalty League and sheriff's deputies rounded up 1,200 Mexican males for deportation at gunpoint. Irish-American Mike Foudy later recalled that the men "were herded out of their homes . . . into boxcars . . . [and] dumped in the desert like a bunch of animals . . . [just because] the companies didn't want a union."[19]

The Bisbee action was only one of many assaults against Mexicans and pro-union workers. The 1917 Espionage Act and 1918 Sedition Act were used to jail or deport trade unionists by the hundreds. Federal troops raided IWW headquarters, patrolled freight cars for Mexican migrant activists, and swept through mining camps intimidating pro-union forces. In 1918 the IWW's top 101 leaders were convicted on trumped-up conspiracy charges. Some of the best champions of labor's cause were sent off to jail.

After Russian troops withdrew from the war effort against Germany to support the Bolshevik (Communist) Revolution of 1917, a new spirit of anticommunism fueled the jingoism (extreme belligerent nationalism). Labeling labor organizers "Red" equated them with disloyal Americans.

Despite this effort to discredit the most able leaders, the dynamic labor movement won shorter hours in several states and even a child labor law in 1919, the same year women won the vote. Nonetheless, most African Americans and Latinos were denied the ballot by various ruses (see chapter 6), and the child labor law did not cover farmworkers. Latino children continued to work alongside their parents in the fields.

In the summer of 1919, as the troops returned home from the bloody war that had cost so many lives, white veterans took back their jobs from the Mexican immigrants, women, and others who had kept production going. President Wilson had told the public that the war was being fought to "make the world safe for democracy." African-American, Mexican-American, and Puerto Rican war veterans, like everyone else, had embraced that noble cause. Now the veterans demanded an end to discrimination, desegregation of public facilities, and equal voting rights and job opportunities.

Ku Klux Klansmen and other white racists had their own definition of democracy—freedom for only white

Americans. Mobs stormed through African-American neighborhoods, attacking homes, pulling women and children off buses, clubbing, shooting, and lynching. To defend themselves and their families, veterans fought back. Twenty-six cities, including the nation's capital, became war zones with the sounds of gunfire crackling for nights on end. Washington D.C.'s riot was triggered by 200 sailors and marines trying to find and lynch a couple of African-American youths accused of "jostling" a naval officer's wife. Navy officers and elected officials did nothing to stop them.[20]

With wartime prices remaining sky-high in the postwar period and calls for wartime "patriotism" no longer applicable, in the years 1919–1920, four million workers conducted 2,665 strikes.[21] When Mexican and other steelworkers struck the Chicago-Calumet steel complex, President Wilson broadened exemptions from immigration restrictions to allow employers to import and use hungry, uninformed workers from Mexico to break the strike.

The "Red Scare" was also revived. Workers were told that evil communists were inspiring them to organize and strike. During the Palmer Raids, named after Attorney General A. Mitchell Palmer, lawmen broke into the homes of thousands of suspected "Reds," many of them Jewish, Italian, Spanish, and Latino labor activists, and deported them back to Europe and the Caribbean or Mexico. Socialists elected to state legislatures and the U.S. Congress were denied their seats. New laws labeling labor unions as criminal conspiracies were enacted by several states, including California. All of these measures, combined with increased deportations of Mexican strikers at gunpoint in the West and Midwest, brought to an end the decades of labor militancy and introduced a period of so-called normalcy—the 1920s.

Many working people realized that if they were ever to win a national eight-hour-day law, a living wage, and genuine democratic representation, they would have to keep on organizing. That proved difficult in the 1920s, especially for African Americans, Latinos, and swarthy southern and eastern European immigrants. It was the heyday of the eugenics movement, when half the states passed sterilization laws applicable to people who were called genetically inferior—often darker-skinned individuals deemed criminal or mentally retarded. Books and magazine articles described Latinos as a "eugenic menace," "inferior," even "born communist."[22] The *New York Times* reported that "the killings of Mexicans [in Texas] without provocation is so common as to pass almost unnoticed."[23]

The 1924 Immigration Act established a quota system that slammed the door on most of the immigrants, guaranteeing the predominance of supposedly genetically superior white people from Northern Europe. A border-patrol-guarded door at the Mexican-U.S. border was left open for Mexicans, since they were so desperately needed in agriculture.

As citizens, of course, Puerto Ricans could still enter the country. Estimates of their numbers on the mainland ranged from 50,000 to 200,000 by 1930. Most headed for New York, hoping to find decent jobs but ending up scrubbing floors and toilets, working twelve-hour shifts in dangerous garment sweatshops, and picking crops on farms in New Jersey and Long Island.

When the worldwide Great Depression took hold in the 1930s, more than 12 million people were thrown out of work, many of them Latinos. Unable to meet rent payments, families were evicted from their homes, their possessions piled up on sidewalks and along roadsides. People marched, holding up signs reading "We Want Food."

Looking for someone to blame, some unemployed white workers targeted Latinos in a new "brown scare." An article in a prominent magazine was headlined "Welcome Paupers and Crime: Puerto Rico's Shocking Gift to the U.S."[24] Puerto Ricans in New York City's East Harlem, El Barrio, rallied to protest these slurs and to demand jobs, housing, and food. They joined with others, mostly Italian Americans and Jews, to elect a pro-labor, antiracist Italian American—Vito Marcantonio—as their congressman in 1934. Nicknamed "Puerto Rico's congressman," Marcantonio was reelected in 1938 and served until 1950.[25]

Once more there were mass deportations. This time authorities rounded up between 400,000 and 1 million "illegal alien" (and sometimes U.S.-born) Latinos, mostly Mexicans. The suffering and fear in Latino families became hard to bear, but still they struggled on. As soon as one group of Mexican pro-union "troublemakers" (as the authorities called them) was deported, another group was brought in to break a strike or pick the crops. Employers imported up to a half million Mexican workers during the 1930s.

As conditions grew worse for *all* working people, the tricks of pitting one group of workers against another were less successful and talk of unions spread. Once again, strike waves rolled across the land. Florida's Cuban tobacco workers struck in 1931. Not long afterward, Puerto Rican, Mexican, and other Latina garment workers on the West Coast joined Jewish-American and Italian-American women of the thirty-year-old International Ladies Garment Workers Union (ILGWU) to carry out major strikes. Cannery workers, packers, and pecan and walnut shellers, mostly Latina, also struck.

In 1935–1936, striking American workers won the Wagner Act establishing a National Labor Relations Board (NLRB) that gave unions legal status. Sit-ins in the rubber, auto, and other industries, where workers refused to leave the plants, won this and additional concessions. The strikers in the industrial plants forced the organized wing of the labor movement to take a giant step forward: the creation of the CIO (Congress of Industrial Organizations). The CIO unionized across industry instead of by craft. For the first time, when an industrial strike was called, *every* worker regardless of job category, from operatives to skilled

Cuban women working in a cigar factory

machinists, joined together on the picket lines. The CIO later merged with the craft-based AFL (American Federation of Labor) to become today's AFL-CIO. Both the NLRB and the CIO worked to stabilize the growing labor unrest. They established collective bargaining arrangements to assure basic union rights.

Although dominated by whites, the CIO relied heavily on nonwhite workers. For example, the 125,000-strong

A Latina working in a factory

United Cannery, Agricultural, Packing, and Allied Workers of America was the CIO's seventh largest union in 1938. It had a majority Latina and female membership, as well as several Latina leaders.[26]

Latinos were active in most of the major strikes of the 1930s. They were among the longshoremen who sparked the famous 1934 San Francisco general strike—a work stoppage by almost every worker in the city, which was violently ended by the army. By 1937, Latinos achieved leadership positions in the newly founded International Longshoremens and Warehousemens Union (ILWU) and many CIO locals. During a unionization drive among the "Little Steel" companies (smaller companies), Mexican Americans made up three-fourths of the pickets at East Chicago's Inland Steel plants in 1937. Mexican-American trade unionists and their families from South Chicago's barrios were among those heading up that year's peaceful, pro-union Memorial Day parade when the Chicago police opened fire, killing ten and wounding more than a hundred.[27]

Despite all the suffering, the Latinos' decades of struggle for a decent life were not in vain. Their help in building the labor movement finally won the eight-hour day in 1938. Other laws introduced in the late 1930s by President Franklin D. Roosevelt's administration established a minimum wage, created the Social Security system, mandated unemployment insurance and workmen's compensation benefits, and banned child labor.

After Japan bombed Pearl Harbor in December 1941, the government ordered the incarceration of the nation's 100,000 Japanese Americans and declared war on Germany, Italy, and Japan. German and Italian Americans were never interned, although some of them openly supported the fascists. To arm Great Britain and the Soviet Union, already fighting Hitler's war machine for more than a year, the country's armaments plants had long been humming at full capacity, putting unemployed people back to work. Now, as young men again went off to war, labor shortages developed.

Mexican "braceros" were contracted to keep the railroads running and the food industry producing. The Mexicans made a great contribution to the wartime defense of American democracy (see chapters 1 and 6). White women and some nonwhites were hired by factories. African Americans and Latinos, however, were still "the last to be hired and the first to be fired." The 6,000-strong Spanish-Speaking Peoples Congress, known as El Congreso, protested discriminatory hiring practices in the defense industry.

Founded in 1938 by Guatemalan-born Luisa Moreno, a former New York City seamstress, El Congreso embraced the wartime slogan "Americans All." But it was unable to persuade the government to create job training programs for more than a few Latinos.

The Allies were fighting to beat back the most terrifying racists of all time—the Nazis—but racism continued at home. In 1943 sailors and marines on leave in Oakland and Los Angeles, looking for excitement, invaded the Mexican-American and African-American ghettoes and beat up on people they called "greasers and niggers." Filipinos were also attacked, since they "looked Japanese," according to the rioters. Many of the victims were called zoot-suiters, because of the distinctive pegged pants and long jackets they wore. Once again, as in 1919, marines and naval officers did nothing to discourage the outbreaks of violence.[28]

Overseas, Latino and African-American soldiers experienced much more respect and equal treatment from Europeans than their families were receiving at home. When the veterans returned home, they joined together with other workers to demand fair treatment. To support the fight against fascism, union members had agreed to wage freezes for the duration of the conflict. As a result, corporate profits steadily rose. Now, with the war over, the unions asked for wage hikes to "catch up." When most employers refused, workers struck in larger numbers and more industries than ever before. Employers conceded substantial wage hikes to get all the strikers back to work.

But a new problem quickly became apparent. If the war plants shut down, unemployment might shoot right back up to the levels of the 1930s. A new "enemy" had to be found to make sure the wheels of the defense industry kept spinning. The time had come again to play the Red Scare card. The Communist Soviet Union, the nation's ally in the war, was suddenly portrayed as the enemy—even though 20 million of its citizens had been killed during the war and most of its armaments factories had been bombed.

In the name of the Cold War against the threat of Communism, politicians and employers mounted a terrifying witch-hunt known as McCarthyism. Thousands of people were dismissed from their jobs on the grounds that they were national security risks or once "knew or associated with communists." The accused were given no opportunity to face their accusers.

Organized labor's most capable leaders were especially targeted in the name of fighting communism. Many of the Latinos' best organizers lost their jobs or, as in the case of Luisa Moreno, were deported. Another leader of the Spanish-Speaking People's Congress, Josefina Fierro de Bright, fled the United States rather than provide the House Un-American Activities Committee with the names of friends or acquaintances whom the inquisitors claimed were "guilty by association with known communists." A new anti-labor law called the Taft-Hartley Act was passed that placed severe restrictions on union organizing and the right to strike. Free speech was curtailed through intimidation. The 1950s became known as the silent fifties.[29]

Only a few brave souls continued the labor struggle. In Detroit, where 5,000 Mexican Americans made up half the workforce at Great Lakes Steel, Latinos in the Latin-

American Steelworkers' Club called for equal access to jobs and housing. Out West, the Asociación Nacional México-Americana (ANMA), founded by New Mexico miners in 1949 after a clash with police, fought for multiracial unity.

ANMA's backbone was "Mine-Mill"—the International Union of Mine, Mill and Smelter Workers founded by descendants of the copper miners who had sparked the great mining strikes of 1903–1919. Three-quarters of copper production workers in the Southwest were Mine-Mill members. In 1952, the union won a now famous fifteen-month strike against Empire Zinc in New Mexico. The courage of Latina pickets who took up the struggle after their husbands were jailed helped turn the tide to victory. The film *Salt of the Earth*, banned during the McCarthy period, told the story of the strike. In 1954, when the government launched "Operation Wetback" (see chapter 1), ANMA courageously defended the deportees. By 1955, however, ANMA was witch-hunted out of existence.[30]

The witch-hunt died down after Senator Joseph McCarthy overreached himself and investigated the U.S. Army for suspected communists. By then, technological advances made during wartime were changing the lives of most Americans. As Cold War armament manufacturing and the new atomic bomb industry boomed, other factories operated around the clock churning out television sets, automobiles, refrigerators, and new appliances and gadgets never before available. Home building, financed with government loans to veterans and others, kept thousands of construction workers busy year-round. Restaurants, hotels, travel agencies, and other small businesses mushroomed, as air travel became common and tourism increased enormously. "Affluent America" was born.

There was still plenty of dirty work to be done, though, and as usual Latinos, kept out of the better-paying occupations, found work as laborers, restaurant workers, and a myriad of other less desirable jobs. Operation Bootstrap encouraged the outmigration of hundreds of thousands of Puerto Ricans to the East Coast of the United States. The new arrivals fanned out to cities throughout the Northeast and Midwest and found work that Anglos didn't want.

The lives of Latinos had improved, but seeing the way the rest of America lived, they felt no better off. Most continued to live in the worst urban slums, kept out of the new suburban housing by discrimination and lack of money. Ugly housing projects rimmed their barrios, hiding them from traffic passing through on superhighways leading to all-white suburbs.

African Americans too, especially in the South, were making very little progress against discrimination and its devastating economic impact until they began organizing the powerful civil rights movement in the mid-1950s. Their struggles and hard-won victories shook the nation and had a profound effect on Latinos.

What African Americans had long called the talented tenth—the minority of people in any group who have extraordinary talent—used the 1960s' antidiscrimination legislation and President Johnson's War on Poverty programs to advance themselves. For almost the first time, Latinos began to enter the professions. Prosperous whites began to meet the "invisible minorities" in the ranks of the better-paid workforce and at the nation's colleges (see chapters 4 and 5).

Starting in 1973, an economic decline aggravated the disease of racism. A white backlash against affirmative action hiring practices limited the number of Latinos and African Americans finally able to "make it." The mass media played on white people's job insecurities and fears by exaggerating nonwhite urban crime, narcotics trafficking, and gang warfare.

As America's post-World War II economic affluence tapered off after Japan's and Western Europe's economic recovery and the end of the costly Vietnam War in 1975, it became fashionable not only to scapegoat minorities but also to blame the unions for the nation's supposed lack of competitiveness. In actuality, American companies were moving overseas to take advantage of wages a fraction of those paid here. *No* American, unionized or not, would ever accept a Brazilian or Mexican wage of 6 dollars *a day!*

The most industrialized nation in the world was rapidly deindustrializing, as the economy shifted over to banking, marketing, and other services. Hi-tech computerization and robotics required fewer workers and therefore fewer labor costs. Many college-educated Americans began cracking bitter jokes about their future careers of "Mcjobs"—low-wage service work like selling hamburgers at McDonald's.

Union members understandably grew disillusioned with their often corrupt leadership that dated its origins to the men who replaced the so-called "communists" during the McCarthy witch-hunt. Under fire from every side, unions saw their membership plummet from a third of the workforce to less than one-fifth (about 15 percent today). Even Cesar Chavez's popular UFW saw its membership drop by half. It had taken almost a century of struggle to build the unions and only thirty years to cripple them!

When Ronald Reagan became president in 1981, he ordered a halt to the unionized air traffic controllers' PATCO strike and allowed the permanent replacement of strikers with nonunion labor. The campaign against the unions seemed to be entering its "final solution" phase.

Amidst growing concern over the nation's economic hard times, an old story reappeared. Latinos and others, most of them far too young to remember the successful days of the CIO, decided that the only way to improve their lives was by organizing a new union movement. New York City's independent 100,000-member District 1199 hospital and health workers' union, now led by Dennis Rivera, represented the spirit of the "new unionism" (a revitalized union movement).

Starting with a hard-fought, victorious twenty-one-month strike against the Farah Clothing Company in the early 1970s, Latina women began talking union. In 1991, Latina workers united with others to strike Diamond Walnut in Texas. The company had just announced its highest profits in history, made possible by the workers' earlier acceptance of wage cuts. Diamond dismissed the strikers and brought in permanent replacement workers. The victimized employees promptly launched a consumers' boycott against Diamond products. "Can nuts, not people!" they joked on their picket lines. They lobbied Congress for a law to prohibit permanent replacement of striking workers.

Other Latinos, drawing a lesson from the UFW experience, decided it was time to organize the unorganized. While all the media's and politicians' union-bashing was going on, they were helping "undocumented aliens," mostly farmworkers, win several strikes (see chapter 1).

Older unions also began admitting the undocumented workers into their ranks. By 1985, "illegals" (as the undocumented immigrants were called) accounted for a third of the Teamsters' Los Angeles membership. In 1991 the new unionism's reformers, Teamsters for a Democratic Union, won the elections of the International Brotherhood of Teamsters. Their reform slate included the first Latino ever to sit on the Teamsters executive board.[31]

Latino copper miners affiliated with the United Steelworkers of America struck yet again in the Clifton-Morenci area of Arizona. They were protesting Phelps Dodge's attempts to destroy their thirteen unions. When a court injunction barred strikers from the mine gates, the miners' wives and daughters began picketing, just as Latinas had done in New Mexico, decades earlier. An Arizona policeman complained: "If we could just get rid of those broads, we'd have it made." The strike eventually petered out and Phelps Dodge shut down much of production, but strikers won several suits against the company.[32]

In New York City, people feared a modern-day Triangle Shirtwaist fire when nonunion apparel sweatshops worked by Dominicans and other recent immigrants sprang up in ancient loft buildings. In Los Angeles and other cities, Central Americans and Mexicans worked for abysmal wages in dangerous subcontracted workshops for the big auto companies and other manufacturers. When Latinos talked union, the ILGWU (International Ladies Garment Workers Union) and UAW (United Auto Workers) began organizing them.

In the mid-1990s, a quarter of the nation's children still went to bed hungry every night. Many of them were African American and Latino. Few participants in the new unionism had ever heard of the 1903 Clifton-Morenci strike or the 1930s' Little Steel strikes that had helped win a better life for millions of Americans—but their feet were marching in the same direction.

Latinos and other Americans who knew a little history hoped that today's parents and their older children would be able to accomplish what so many of their great-great-grandparents had done. This time, they hoped, the fight to build a decent work life would lead to more comfortable circumstances for *all* the nation's working people—and for more than one generation!

cuatro

STRUGGLING

FOR

BETTER

SCHOOLS

*I told the counselor I wanted to go to college,
but she said, "Have you thought about beauty
college?" Beauty college! That's all she thinks
we're good for.*
        —Latina high school student,
        Dallas, Texas, 1970s

*Anyways, she hated us to speak Spanish, so I
spoke up. "I was born a Mexican and I was
blessed to speak two languages." She replied,
"I'm sorry you were born a Mexican."*
        —California high school dropout and
        gang member, 1980s.[1]

In 1965 a graduate student researching public education entered a typical elementary school in a semi-rundown multiracial neighborhood of New York City. In the third grade classroom, where the plaster was peeling from the walls, at least half the students looked Latino to him.

The teacher, whose real name the researcher disguised as Miss Dwight, was upset by the way her thirty-three students sang "The Star Spangled Banner." Spanish-speaking children mispronounced words like "ramparts" and "perilous." Apparently, it did not matter to her that no one, not even the English-speaking students, had the faintest idea what the words *meant*.

Miss Dwight kept telling the Latino children to repeat the mispronounced words, but they were not doing well. When they grew frustrated and muttered in Spanish, she shouted:

"Don't speak in Spanish! No Spanish! No Spanish! English, English, English!"

During the math lessons, Miss Dwight continued correcting mispronunciations, getting angrier by the minute when a few students explained they did not *understand* what the words in the addition and subtraction examples *meant*. Assuming they would never understand anything since their achievement test scores were so low, Miss Dwight rapidly read to Mario a subtraction question one more time:

"If six ducks were swimming in a pond and three swam away, how many were left, Mario?"

The teacher sounded angry and the words came at him so rapid-fire that Mario ducked his head and fidgeted in his chair. Miss Dwight sternly hushed one or two other children who tried to help Mario out by whispering *patos* for ducks, *nadando* for swimming, *quedaron* for left. Fortunately, Mario, a neatly dressed dark-skinned boy who just two months earlier had arrived from the Dominican Republic, heard the whispers and proudly answered, "*Tres!*"

"No Spanish! No Spanish!" Miss Dwight shouted. "In *English*, Mario! Now repeat after me: three."

Excitedly and hopefully, Mario said: "OK, teacha, *tree*." (The sound "th" does not exist in Latin American Spanish.)

"Not tree, three!"

Miss Dwight went back and forth with Mario—three/tree, three/tree—and finally gave up. The other boys and girls burst into laughter, but Mario had no idea why anything was so funny or what he was doing wrong. He knew he had done poorly on the achievement test—he barely recognized a few words! Now this!

Miss Dwight called on Marvin to answer the next problem and he gave the correct answer immediately. On the classroom bulletin board were student test papers arranged alphabetically. Marvin's papers were marked with bright gold stars next to Mario's, which were marked with big red Xs.

Over coffee in the teachers' room, Miss Dwight fumed to her friends Edith and Mary: "What really bothers me is all the talking in Spanish. And I'll flip if just one more child calls me 'teacha' today."

"Yeah," said Edith, "when they speak Spanish, they really prattle like monkeys. I'm sure they're not even trying to learn English."

"Wait," said Mary. "Remember that Spanish is natural to them. How would you like the pressure of learning a new language and new subjects all at the same time?"

"Mary," said Edith, "you're entirely too sympathetic. You live in a dream world. Do you really think for one minute that these kids will ever amount to anything? . . . They act like animals too. All you see in the newspapers are gang wars, dope addicts, and rapes."[2]

If things were tough for Mario, they were as bad or worse for Latinos in other cities—and still are. For decades, stereotyping of Latinos has tracked them into classes for "slow kids," not college-bound. The famous Coleman Report on *Equality of Educational Opportunity* in the 1960s found that Puerto Rican children were about three years behind average white children in verbal ability, math, and reading comprehension and one year behind black children. Coleman's tests revealed a deep sense of despair that prevents Latino children from achieving their potential. Daily exposure to stereotyping, like the incidents listed below, gives them a feeling of rejection and helplessness:

- A phys ed instructor noticed that one of the girls was wearing a new gym suit. "Oh," he said loudly, "did the welfare check come?"
- A little girl couldn't wait to get her first report card. But when she got it there was nothing written on it except two big letters: "LD." Language Difficulty.[3]

Most Latino parents never had a chance like the graduate student to observe what was being done to their children at school. But they knew in their hearts there was something terribly wrong. In Milwaukee, for example, a mother complained:

> *They pass the kids just to get rid of them. . . .*
> *But the child has to be educated before he can*
> *get anything . . . if he goes every day to school and*
> *doesn't get anything, he knows he's not*
> *getting educated. He'll drop out. Who's going*
> *to get blamed? The youth.*[4]

Latinos also suspected that many school administrators had the same prejudiced attitudes the teachers expressed in private. They were determined to change the situation.

In the 1930s, Latino families protested the unfair way achievement and literacy tests were used to malign their children. They campaigned against an unscrupulous New York State Chamber of Commerce report that claimed Puerto Rican children were "mentally deficient." The report was based on intelligence test scores in English designed for middle-class white children. Parents at the time demanded bilingual education. A good portion of the later civil rights movement was about precisely this kind of cultural bias in testing.[5]

The attitudes of teachers like Edith go far back in American history. Generations of Latinos were deluged by a tidal wave of prejudice that swept over their children from an early age, tracking them into a life of dead-end jobs or worse. It was almost a miracle if a Latino ever went on to college.

Ironically, in the mid-nineteenth century when there were not yet many public schools, the invading Anglos actually encouraged bilingualism in the Southwest. The California Constitution of 1849 mandated printing laws in Spanish and English, and the Colorado Territory legislated bilingualism in education. They did this for reasons of political expediency. "I had fifteen pupils not one of whom knew any English, and I knew nothing of Spanish," said Elizabeth Post, a schoolteacher in Ehrenberg, Arizona, in 1872.[6]

Once the newcomers to the Southwest consolidated their power, however, they introduced "no Spanish" and "English only" laws and a segregated school system. Mexican Americans had to attend separate schools for Mexicans. If there were none, Latinos received no education at all. In predominantly Latino El Paso, Texas, there was no "Mexican" high school until 1927. Textbooks omitted Latino culture and history and emphasized education about Anglo traditions. Because voting rights for Latinos were practically nonexistent, not a single Latino was elected to a state superintendent of schools position in the Southwest between 1850 and 1900. In sum, education for Latinos, most of whom could not afford private school tuition, was "exclusionary, discriminatory, and assimilationist," according to one expert.[7]

By the start of the twentieth century, when public schools began to appear in every corner of the land, Latinos found themselves almost completely shut out. Not until 1982 (*Plyler* v. *Doe*) did the Supreme Court rule *against* exclusion from public schools of millions of children of undocumented immigrants.[8]

During all those many decades parents fought back in every barrio of the nation, both for access to public schooling and for better education—including the use of Spanish where appropriate. In Puerto Rico, generations of students resented the English-only law for school instruction imposed after the U.S. takeover of the island. Good sense finally prevailed fifty years later—in 1948, when the schools switched back to Spanish.

Long before the civil rights movement, barrio residents fought against English-only laws, some of which were repealed by the courts as early as the 1920s. They also fought against being segregated into inferior schools that looked like outhouses or garages instead of the nice-looking new public schools. Even in Texas, where anti-Latino racism was particularly intense, they refused to accept the idea that their kids were going to be put into a shack.

The parents launched lawsuits and won the nation's *first* court cases ordering school desegregation. Their initial victory occurred in 1931 in a small Mexican rural community in affluent Lemon Grove outside San Diego, California. Mexican Americans had been living there since the turn of the century. Most worked at the fruit orchards, a local mining quarry, the railroad, or as servants in the homes of the ricos (rich).

Word quickly spread when a local newspaper described a new grammar school being built in the community: "A fine new building . . . that offers every facility of the well equipped schools." In January, the school principal stood at the door of the completed building to order seventy-five mostly Mexican-American children who had attended the old grammar school to go to a two-room structure nearby. The parents refused to send their children to the building they called *la caballeriza* (the barnyard).

Instead, risking job loss and in some cases deportation, they appealed to the Mexican consul for legal help and went to the courts. They also gained support from the Spanish-language press and other Latinos in San Diego. California legislators tried to push through a law legalizing school segregation. White racists harassed Lemon Grove's Latino parents and children. On March 30, 1931, the judge ruled in favor of the Mexican Americans. Guitar playing, singing, and dancing lasted long into the night![9]

It turned out to be an isolated victory. LULAC (League of United Latin American Citizens, founded in 1929) lost several similar suits in Texas during the 1930s.[10] Often LULAC followed the lead of community activists like those of Lemon Grove.

LULAC members were successful middle-class and professional Latinos, mostly Mexican Americans, determined to assimilate into the dominant Anglo culture and fulfill "the American dream." LULAC and the NAACP (National Association for the Advancement of Colored People, founded in 1910), are the nation's oldest, most enduring civil rights organizations. They have always believed in going through the courts to fight racial segregation and bigotry.

But the courts invariably moved slowly. After the Lemon Grove victory in 1931, it took until 1946–1947 for LULAC and the NAACP to win a school desegregation case in southern California's Westminster school district and other districts of Orange County. A federal court ruled that segregating Mexican-American children on the basis of language difference could not be justified past the early grades and violated the Fourteenth Amendment "equal protection" clause. A 1948 U.S. district court case in Texas ruled in the same fashion. Both cases paved the way for the famous *Brown* v. *Board of Education* decision of 1954 outlawing racial segregation in the nation's public schools.[11]

The Brown decision came about because of the political pressures of changing times. The successful anticolonial revolutions of the peoples of Africa and Asia and the overthrow of U.S.-supported dictatorships in Latin America after World War II made ongoing racial segregation a national embarrassment. Returning African-American and Latino war veterans, having fought overseas for democracy, angrily denounced its absence at home. President Truman issued an executive order to end racial segregation in the armed forces. Veterans of the Korean War kept up the antiracism pressure.

As McCarthyism waned in the late 1950s, Latinos stepped up their efforts to improve education. In 1959, LULAC gained state funding in Texas for its Little School of 400 program introduced to teach preschoolers some basic English. It became a model for the federally funded Head Start program that soon followed. The Council of Puerto Rican and Spanish Organizations of Greater New York, founded in 1952, conducted marches against "Jim Crow" school segregation responsible for inferior schools.[12]

The civil rights movement sounded the death knell of McCarthyism and ended the political silence of the early 1950s. The African Americans' many peaceful marches in the deep South in the face of savage dogs, water hoses, police beatings, and night-rider murders "awakened the conscience of this nation."[13] An immediate result was the 1964 Civil Rights and Economic Opportunity acts.

Latinos and others gained inspiration and hope from the examples of African Americans courageously challenging the way things had always been done. Equally inspiring was the example of the brave Latino farmworkers discussed in chapter 1. High school and college youth swung into motion. In the fall of 1964 the young Mexican-American folksinger and pacifist Joan Baez led University of California-Berkeley students of the FSM (Free Speech Movement) up the steps of Sproul Hall to occupy it and demand what the students termed "freedom classes." Growing numbers of activists, not just adults but students, began clamoring for an overhaul of the nation's educational system.[14]

Despite the 1964 Civil Rights Act ending discrimination in public accommodations in the South, poor Latinos and other deprived groups in the North and West saw little immediate change. In 1965, in the Watts ghetto of Los Angeles, African Americans took to the streets. Attacked by police, they reacted angrily. Most of the neighborhood went up in flames. President Lyndon Johnson promptly initiated a War on Poverty, funding job-training programs and many community agencies that momentarily put quite a few minority people to work.

To some, even these efforts seemed like tokenism, not substantive change, and too little too late. In 1966, as black civil rights marchers pushed forward with cries of "black power," Latino youth began substituting direct action for LULAC's go-slow approach. They and other powerless groups also took to the streets to demand changes that would increase their chances to have a meaningful share of power.

Younger Mexican Americans started calling themselves "Chicanos," a term traditionally used by the working class to refer to itself and one that richer Mexican Americans used negatively against the lower class. Some Chicano activists cited the 1848 Treaty of Guadalupe Hidalgo (see chapter 1) as a legal basis for bilingualism and cultural maintenance. The new generation emphasized its roots in *la raza*—the race of Mexicans and Native Americans who had resisted Spanish and U.S. colonialism.

After a young man named Rodolfo "Corky" Gonzales, son of migrant farmworkers, and other Mexican Americans stormed out of a 1966 federal jobs conference in New Mexico, President Johnson finally acknowledged that Latinos, and not just African Americans, had legitimate gripes. Gonzales then founded the Denver-based Crusade for Justice that organized marches to end discrimination in the schools and lawmen's violence against Latinos.[15]

In light of renewed mass marches and urban uprisings after Watts, Congress passed the 1968 Civil Rights Act expanding earlier legislation. It also implicitly recognized the link of unfair housing to unfair schooling by passing the Fair Housing Act. People pressed for implementation of these programs and an end to the escalating Vietnam War (see chapter 6).

On the morning of March 3, 1968, shouts of "Blow Out!" rang out in the halls of Abraham Lincoln High School in the Mexican-American barrio of East Los Angeles. Teacher Sal Castro, a Korean War veteran who had gone to college on the GI bill, led 1,000 students in a walkout, demanding better education. Castro and the students wanted more Mexican-American teachers, staff, and curriculum content; freedom of speech; and an end to white racist practices at the city's schools. Lawmen rushed to the scene and began beating the youths. As word spread to five other barrio schools, thousands more Chicano students walked out. The Los Angeles "blow-outs," involving 10,000 participants, lasted a week and a half and soon spread to the rest of the West and Midwest.

Student and youth organizations formed. The main ones included the United Mexican American Students, the Mexican American Youth Organization, and the college-based *El Movimiento Estudiantil Chicano de Aztlán* (MECHA—The Chicano Student Movement of Aztlán, after the mythical name for the pre-Mexico, pre-U.S. lands). A 5,000-strong youth militia of young Chicano women and men, the Brown Berets, stood ready to defend the community against police violence. Hundreds trekked to Denver in 1969 for the First National Chicano Youth Liberation Conference.[16]

The mood became militant among Puerto Ricans too. Chicago's Puerto Rican street gangs buried the hatchet and founded the Young Lords. Students linked up with the Lords, and new Young Lords chapters emerged. Some, like New York City's, were predominantly student based. The Lords issued militant manifestos and set up community service programs (see chapter 2).

Both the Brown Berets and the Young Lords were

*Brown Berets (a Latino self-defense group)
help carry the casket of a friend.*

influenced by the Black Panthers, founded in Oakland, California, as an African-American self-defense group in 1967. In Chicago, the Lords formed a multiracial rainbow coalition with the Panthers and the Young Patriots—white migrant youth from the Appalachian Mountains. Talk of multiracial unity spread.

Both puzzled and inspired by the audacity of the youth, Latino parents worked even harder than before to tear down the barriers to a good education. Because of the civil rights movement of the 1960s they began to succeed, so that a few more Marios might have a chance to escape the rut of poverty. Because of their and others' efforts, more poor children of *all* races had a chance to receive a decent education, maybe even attend college someday—at least in the 1970s.

Because of the hard-fought passage of the 1968 Civil Rights Act and its ban on discrimination based on national origin (Title VII), Latinos had a "window of opportunity" to push for more bilingualism in the schools. Under pressure, Congress finally passed the underfunded Equal Educational Opportunity Act of 1974, mandating bilingual programs.

After more court suits that same year, the U.S. Supreme Court ruled that California had violated the equal protection clause of the 1964 Civil Rights Act by depriving children with a limited grasp of English of their rights to public education. The justices forbade English-only instruction. By the late 1970s and early 1980s, the nation's Latino students, using the partly opened window, were closing the gap in test scores separating them from whites, even in math and science. Their math scores improved by as much as 45 percent.[17]

By the early 1970s, many Chicanos and Puerto Ricans were beginning to employ the word "Latino" to identify their common struggle. By building mass movements in the streets they won further concessions, including the 1975

Voting Rights Act calling for the bilingual ballot (see chapter 6, on guaranteeing rights).

There were problems and mistakes, of course. Demands for more nonwhite teachers occasionally led to confrontations—pushing and shoving—and escalated into demands for *replacing* white teachers with Latinos or blacks. Demands for more community control over local schools rose to feverish heights, and continue today. The basic reasoning used then is still applied: "If the school remains alien to the values and needs of the community, if it is bureaucratically run, then the children will not receive the education they are entitled to, no matter what language they are taught in."[18]

After the long years of struggle, today the same graduate student who visited Miss Dwight's class would more readily find a few examples of how a better third grade might work. In Kansas City, a Mexican-American woman—we'll call her Elena—contrasts with the Edith we met earlier. Elena teaches at a magnet school, an experimental one given extra resources and staff to draw students from a broad area and see if, under the best of circumstances, academic achievement will improve.

In Elena's classroom are thirty-five students, some of them Latinos. One we'll call María has enrolled late because her family just moved from Mexico. Elena greets María in Spanish and hands her some books. "Now you're going to learn two languages, María," she says. "Most people only speak one!" María smiles and feels proud. Later in the day, María is learning science. To introduce new concepts Elena speaks in both English and Spanish. Then she continues in English for the actual work. It is hard at first, but María quickly catches on. The teacher is helpful and considerate. In Elena's class no one mocks or embarrasses a child who stumbles in English.

In all María's classes she meets people from different races and backgrounds, many of whom know little or no

Spanish. She makes friends with some of them. Para-professionals—paid teachers' aides or unpaid Latina mothers lending volunteer time—assist the children in bilingual reading, writing, arithmetic, and science classes. In the months ahead, achievement scores, including María's, steadily improve.[19]

The magnet schools like the one in Kansas City offer a wonderful opportunity but have never been extended widely around the country. After visiting several cities in the late 1980s, education expert Jonathan Kozol found magnet schools were usually:

> *disproportionately white and middle class. . . .*
> *The poorest parents . . . lack the information access*
> *and the skills of navigation in an often hostile and*
> *intimidating situation to channel their children*
> *to the better schools.*[20]

Most parents feel that *all* public schools should provide the advantages of the handful of magnet schools. But even in average schools they believe the situation could be markedly improved. In 1993, a middle-aged non-Latina alumna returned to her old grade school in a small city of New York's Hudson River Valley. She saw a number of new students from Latin America. The principal took her to a bilingual science class, where she watched as Latino children who had been enrolled for only a couple of years read aloud from textbooks. Their English was good and they answered questions correctly. Afterward, in the hallway, a history teacher commented: "I wish all my students were as motivated as these [Latino] kids."

At a school in another small city nearby, two-way bilingualism was being used. Teachers worked in teams. One told a visitor:

> *My first graders are all English-speaking, Ana's are*
> *Spanish-speaking. We each teach academic subjects*

to our own classes in their own language. I teach English to her class every day. She teaches Spanish to mine. We mix them for art, music, gym, library, and lunch. They understand each other and pick up books in both languages. It's enriching for both groups. [21]

Schools like these receive financial assistance for bilingual education under federal legislation dating back to the 1960s. Initially, only one group of Latinos had any bilingual programs. They were newly arriving Cuban political refugees favored by government policy makers because they were anticommunists opposed to the 1959 Cuban Revolution (see chapter 6). The government now mandates bilingual instruction for grades where at least twenty students are termed "Limited English Proficient" (LEP) and have the same native language. If the number is smaller, then ESL (English as a Second Language) services must be provided.

ESL programs usually involve smaller, more flexible classes, using simpler words, visual aids, and gestures to teach vocabulary. Rewarding careers have opened up for teachers of ESL, and the nation has become more aware of its rich cultural diversity. But today's bilingual and ESL programs are grossly underfunded, understaffed, the subject of bitter political disputes, and consequently sometimes ineffective. They don't exist in many schools that desperately need them because the census undercounts Latinos.

Even worse, some voters are under the false impression that bilingual programs intend to replace English with Spanish when actually they are meant merely to offer some equity to persons for whom English is difficult or new. In 1986, California's predominantly white electorate passed a referendum rejecting bilingualism. As a result of that vote, some 40,000 immigrants were turned away from ESL classes the in Los Angeles Unified School District. In some other places, local laws mandate "English only," depriving many children of the benefits of bilingual programs. Sadly, about half of the nation's Latino students still are "taught" in classrooms resembling Miss Dwight's. The number of children who could benefit from bilingual programs increased 36 percent between 1986 and 1991 to 2.26 million. In schools where the programs have continued, such as PS 102 in Queens, New York, where thirty-eight languages are spoken, one ESL teacher has noted: "Students learn English quickly so they can talk to one another."[22]

In fact, Latinos are learning English as fast as earlier immigrant groups did. Latino parents realize how important English is for their own and their children's success. U.S. Census Bureau data indicate that 85 to 90 percent of Hispanic Americans and Latino immigrants ages five to seventeen speak English at home. Today's more than 25 million Latinos, about a third of them recent immigrants, are predominantly bilingual.

Most native-born Americans speak only one language. Back in the 1950s, high school students were required to learn a second language in order to graduate. To deal successfully with the realities of today's global economy and our culturally diverse society, knowledge of more than one language is looked upon favorably by business executives, government officials, and educators when they select among job applicants. More years of education are also a valuable asset in the tight employment market. Some 40 percent of all new immigrants from Asia are college graduates—one reason some whites like to call them a "model minority"— but there are hardly any college graduates among the new Latino immigrants. Their early educational experiences and lack of financial resources make it difficult for them to complete high school, let alone enter college.[23]

Over the years, there has developed a huge contradiction between the lofty ideals of the *Brown* decision and the way schools operate in the real world. Most school systems are financed by local property taxes. That means concretely that in poor neighborhoods schools are underfunded, while in better-off areas schools are given much more money.

In 1971 Demetrio Rodríguez went to court to press the issue. The impoverished school district where he lived in San Antonio was 96 percent nonwhite. It spent *one-fif-teenth* per pupil of what a predominantly wealthy and white district spent. A Texas court ruled that Rodríguez had been denied his Fourteenth Amendment right to equal protection. The decision had major implications for the whole nation. Many parents and educators believed that it would mean eventual equal spending for the education of *all* children.

Their hopes were dashed in 1973, when the Supreme Court, by a 5-to-4 margin, overturned the decision, ruling that the U.S. Constitution does not make "fiscal neutrality" in education—in other words, *equal education*—a fundamental right. In his dissent, Justice Thurgood Marshall claimed *Brown* clearly meant education "is a right which must be made available to all on equal terms."[24]

Demetrio Rodríguez continued to pursue his case under Texas state laws, finally winning a unanimous decision by the Texas Supreme Court *sixteen years later*, in 1989! Unfortunately, the legal victory didn't change reality. Because of loopholes in subsequent legislation to correct the problem, the education of poor children in Texas remains the same. Legal loopholes and altered tax laws have diluted the impact of a similar series of court decisions against unequal education in other states—New Jersey in 1988, for example.

Unfortunately, during the 1980s and early 1990s severe budgetary reductions in bilingual education and other social programs closed the "window of opportunity" further. Unfavorable court decisions and a rollback in civil rights enforcement left it open a mere crack. By 1992, for example, New York State's allocation from federal Emergency Immigrant Education Assistance funds was cut *by half* from its already reduced 1990 level. Yet New York's schools enrolled nearly *three* times the usual number of new immigrants.[25]

Educational experts agree that federal programs will never be more than Band-Aids on the sores of inequity unless funding for education is equalized. Some have proposed equal budgeting of all schools from a common federal tax fund. Others say that a program to provide well-paid employment for everyone is the best way to keep local control of the schools and raise the tax bases of poor neighborhoods. Other less direct ways have also been suggested.[26]

Obtaining a quality *college* education is even more difficult for Latinos. Leaders of New York City's Puerto Rican Forum, founded in the 1950s to create career opportunities, realized that access to college was a key part of career advancement. They helped launch Aspira in 1961 to promote higher education for Latinos. In 1968, at the height of the civil rights movement, the nonprofit Ford Foundation, a group of wealthy donors, gave Aspira a grant to create chapters in Chicago, Philadelphia, Newark, and San Juan. Aspira promptly signed up 3,000 youths in leadership clubs.

Texas lawyer Pete Tijerina asked Ford officials for similar help for Mexican Americans. To his surprise, he first had to convince the officials that his people did in fact suffer "police brutality and segregation in schools, denial of fair trials . . . and employment discrimination."[27] Ford finally agreed to a $2.2 million seed grant in 1968 to help create MALDEF—the Mexican American Legal Defense and Education Fund, a major civil rights organization today.

In 1967–1969, Latino youth and their parents from New York City's barrios joined with African Americans, Asian Americans, and others to demand an open admissions policy at the tuition-free city university system. (Under an open admissions policy, the university would admit any applicant with a high school diploma.) Traditionally, culturally biased examinations to determine eligibility had kept enrollments nearly all-white. Students seized the buildings of City College of New York and won their demand. Their movement spread nationally, helping Latinos and others to open the "window of opportunity" much more than a crack.

New educational opportunities opened up for high school graduates who might otherwise never have attended college. College admissions for Latinos and African Americans significantly rose from their near zero level. Several new campuses were created especially for them and for poor white working-class youth. Some, like Rutgers University's multiracial Livingston College campus, became famous for the high quality of their faculty and graduates.

In New York City's South Bronx, Puerto Ricans fought for the creation of today's Eugenio María de Hostos Community College, the nation's first bilingual college. Named after a famed Puerto Rican *independentista*, the college was almost eliminated during the city's 1975–1976 fiscal crisis. A student occupation of Hostos and mass marches to City Hall saved the college at least temporarily. Later, in the 1980s and 1990s, similar mass direct actions throughout the nation delayed or moderated tuition hikes and budget cuts that seriously undermined the earlier gains of Latinos and African Americans.

In the late 1970s some of Latin America's new wave of political refugees fleeing U.S.-supported dictatorships (see chapter 6) founded New York City's *Universidad de los Trabajadores* (Workers' University). This nonprofit education center is a place where immigrant workers can go to improve their English and prepare for the high school equivalency exam. Similar educational centers have sprung up all around the nation.[28]

Today Latinos, like other Americans, are receiving more years of schooling, but the educational gap between Latinos and non-Latinos is widening. Based on statistics from the 1980s and early 1990s, a lesser percentage of Latinos than either African Americans or whites graduate from high school, enter or complete college, or enter or complete graduate school or a professional college. In 1990, Latinos accounted for 5.5 percent of college students, but more than half were in two-year colleges. While the percentage of Latino students in major-city public schools is over 20, the Latino high school dropout rate is an alarming 45 percent—twice the black dropout rate and nearly three times the rate for whites.[29]

When we look at educational data on people over twenty-five years of age, we see how disadvantaged Latinos are. About 21 percent of white people in this age group have college degrees, compared to only 7.1 percent for Mexican Americans and 9.6 percent for Puerto Ricans. In the same age group, about seven times as many Latinos as whites and twice as many Latinos as African Americans have less than five years of school. Their children are often raised in homes without books, a severe educational handicap. With Latinos prominent among the estimated 20 million Americans suffering from hunger, there is little wonder that food purchases take priority over books.[30]

In order to improve income levels Latinos need higher levels of English. Yet to achieve these higher levels, they need more income to be able to upgrade their education. The message is a frustrating one: you must learn more to earn more, but you must first earn more to learn more—a classic Catch-22 double-bind for the majority of Latinos who start out so far behind![31]

Unfortunately, white flight of middle class residents from congested urban areas was part of the post-civil rights movement white backlash. This left inner cities with an even lower tax base for education. The 1990 census showed 45 percent of all Americans living in suburbs, 95 percent of them white. Some of those moving to the most expensive areas hired Latino gardeners, baby-sitters, and maids, usually recent immigrants. The bigotry faced by these new Latinos differed little from the prejudice faced by the Latino children in Miss Dwight's third grade classroom.

For example, in 1993 at the affluent resort town of Seaside, Oregon, most white residents saw nothing wrong in a county sheriff's memo stating that Hispanics "have a greater tolerance for domestic abuse, are known to tolerate sexual relationships that are considered rape here, and . . . are involved in organized crime." An overflow town meeting called by outraged Latino immigrants almost erupted in violence.[32]

In 1991, Jonathan Kozol, an author and authority on public education, denounced the dreadful education offered children in urban African-American and Latino schools. He found that thirty-seven years after *Brown* v. *Board of Education*, particularly outside the South, school segregation had intensified. Most urban schools he visited were "95 to 99 percent nonwhite."[33]

Almost every educational gain for Latinos of the sixties and seventies came under attack in the eighties and nineties, even that of speaking in the Spanish language! An English-only movement made English the official language of sixteen states by 1989, including heavily Latino California, Arizona, Colorado, and Florida.

Not willing to return to the "no-Spanish" rules that historically have victimized them, Latinos have had to fight extra hard to preserve bilingual education. Even an outspoken Hispanic opponent of the new emphasis on cultural diversity, Linda Chavez, former head of the U.S. Civil Rights Commission under President Reagan, has objected to the idea of returning to the past when children were forced "to sink or swim in classes in which they don't understand the language of instruction."[34]

Latinos have recently won several court victories against the English-only statutes, helping to breathe new life into emasculated bilingual programs. In 1993 Latinos convinced Dade County (Miami) commissioners to repeal a 1980 ordinance outlawing the use of Spanish in official business. In Puerto Rico, 100,000 people rallied against a proposal by pro-statehood Governor Pedro Rosselló to make English a co-official language on the island. They further rebuffed the governor in a nonbinding referendum to make Puerto Rico a state.[35]

The ongoing conflict over bilingualism has become intertwined with the question of how to improve public education in general. One improvement Latinos have fought for and begun to win is a more multicultural curriculum, helpful not only for building young Latinos' self-esteem but for educating every American about the diversity of the nation's peoples and cultures. The top educators of California, New York, and many other states have mandated a complete overhaul of public school curricula to reflect cultural diversity. A 1991 report endorsed by the New York State Board of Regents recognized the nation's "current reality . . . [of] racial and ethnic pluralism" and the many "virtues of diversity." It called for a new curriculum from kindergarten through twelfth grade to provide a multicultural, antiracist, and antisexist education.[36]

Immediately, a white backlash developed. Despite their small numbers, nonwhite faculty members were targeted by the opponents of multiculturalism. In the early 1990s, thousands of students carried out public rallies to demand that the University of California-Santa Barbara overturn its rejection of Chicano historian Rodolfo Acuña as the campus's first full-time Chicano studies professor. Numerous scholars from around the nation expressed shock that a minority of Santa Barbara history professors, one of them formerly on the CIA payroll, were able to block Acuña's appointment on the absurd grounds of his "insufficient scholarship." Acuña is one of the nation's foremost scholars, internationally renowned as the main founder and developer of Cal State Northridge's famed Chicano Studies Department, a veritable mecca for researchers. The real reason for rejecting Acuña, as the American Civil Liberties Union pointed out, was his long record of political activism.

If misapplied, politicized, or underfinanced, multicultural education can easily fail. California voters have already reduced the educational budget in that state to the point where it now ranks forty-sixth in money spent on education. Some educators note that short of *every* student mastering a sequence of courses on something like "how to end racism and sexism forever," even the best-financed multicultural curriculum may fall short. Moreover, these educators say, the underlying *economic causes* of bigotry and educational failure will still have to be confronted.[37]

One thing is certain. Latinos will keep up their impressive tradition of fighting to improve the nation's crisis-ridden educational system.

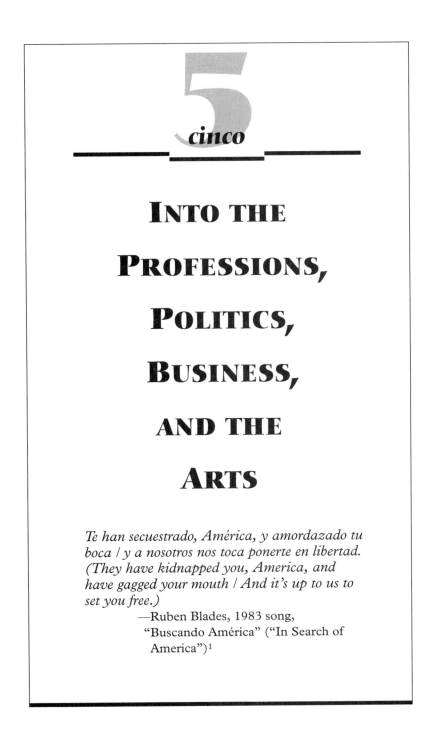

5

cinco

INTO THE

PROFESSIONS,

POLITICS,

BUSINESS,

AND THE

ARTS

Te han secuestrado, América, y amordazado tu boca / y a nosotros nos toca ponerte en libertad. (They have kidnapped you, America, and have gagged your mouth / And it's up to us to set you free.)

—Ruben Blades, 1983 song, "Buscando América" ("In Search of America")[1]

Prior to the passage of the Civil Rights Act of 1964, making it illegal to discriminate on the basis of race, color, religion, sex, or national origin, only a few Latinos were able to secure professional jobs. That fact alone discouraged many young men and women from making the difficult push through college, especially when money was scarce. As a result of the new civil rights legislation, the Equal Employment Opportunity Commission (EEOC) was established to monitor and investigate charges of discrimination on the job market. Affirmative action programs were introduced to remedy the impact of long years of discrimination. They mandated aggressive recruitment of minority personnel, but these requirements were rarely enforced after 1980.[2]

In fact, it took a struggle, often involving court suits, to convince most employers to obey the new laws. A key legal case, *Griggs* v. *Duke Power Company*, led to a 1971 unanimous decision of the Supreme Court forbidding screening procedures to eliminate minority groups. The ruling required "employers to initiate practices that considered their impact on minorities." To avoid costly litigation, the ruling encouraged many employers in public and private sectors to devise programs for the hiring of women and non-Euroamericans. Presidential Executive Order 11246, in 1972, required employers to eliminate "all existing discriminatory conditions whether purposeful or inadvertent" and to take "affirmative action to recruit, employ and promote qualified members or groups formerly excluded."

As a result, there were spurts of new employment for Latinos in the 1970s. Many large business firms, especially those with government contracts, hired Latinos—although usually only a few to comply with the federal guidelines. Often these "token" employees felt isolated in the workplace and were not advanced as rapidly as white employees. Of all the minorities, women benefited the most from affirmative action. Sometimes employers deliberately hired a talented dark-skinned Latina in order to meet three affirmative action criteria with only one salary: black, Hispanic, and female.

With the possibility of decent professional employment opening up, more Latinos began applying to college. The number of Latino college graduates approached 10 percent of Hispanics age 25 years and over by 1991,[3] but as we saw in the previous chapter few attended prestigious four-year colleges.

Just a glance at the shockingly short lists of today's Latino attorneys and law professors reveals the fact that most of them were born in the 1940s and 1950s, benefiting from the affirmative action programs of the 1970s. Even so, only 2 percent of all law students were Latinos in 1985, a mere 1 percent increase in a decade! The only Latino law dean in the United States in the early 1990s was Leo M. Romero, dean of the University of New Mexico Law School, named to that post in 1991. There are less than half as many Latino women attorneys as men.

Latinos who graduate from law school face further difficulties. Before a lawyer is able to practice, a very difficult bar examination must be taken. In California, 61.5 percent of whites passed the July 1985 bar exam but only 33.5 percent of Latinos. Even those who jump through all the hoops are rarely hired by major law firms, which hire largely from the Ivy League or other upper-class colleges.

Through necessity and sometimes preference, therefore, most Latino attorneys end up working for the government or for nonprofit legal organizations and public interest groups—organizations such as the Mexican-American Legal Defense and Education Fund (MALDEF), Migrant Legal Action Program, and other groups that concentrate on aiding the poor. Puerto Rican attorney Wilfredo Caraballo, for example, is a successful public defender working for the State of New Jersey who served as a cabinet member for Governor James Florio from 1990 to 1992. He remains active in the Puerto Rican Legal Defense and Education Fund and enjoys his work because it "gives him an opportunity to deal with the same kinds of public interest problems he faced firsthand as a young man growing up on the streets of Brooklyn and the South Bronx."[4]

Latinos are underrepresented as judges. According to the U.S. Census Bureau, in 1990 there were only 1,098 Latino judges, three-fourths of them male, representing 3.4 percent of the total 32,394. MALDEF, noting that 97 percent of those making the decisions on judiciary appointments are white, calls the judicial appointment system discriminatory. When judges are elected by popular vote, Latinos are more frequently chosen.

Federal judges are appointed by the president. In keeping with antidiscrimination laws, President Jimmy Carter issued an executive order creating a U.S. Circuit Judge Nomination Commission in 1977. With capability as the yardstick, sixteen Latinos were appointed. President Ronald Reagan reverted back to a more traditional appointee system of political favoritism. During his two terms in office only ten Latino federal judges were named. From 1989 to 1991, President George Bush appointed two. There is no Latino Supreme Court justice.

Latinos are even more underrepresented in politics. From the early 1900s until 1950, only five Latino congressmen were elected. The improvement since then has been less than spectacular. The Congressional Hispanic Caucus was founded in December 1976 as a bipartisan group with only twelve members. Fifteen years later, in 1991, ten Latinos held office in Congress. No Latino has been elected to the Senate since 1970. According to the National Association of Hispanic Elected and Appointed Officials, in 1990 there were more than 4,000 Hispanic Americans holding elected office—89 percent of them Democrats. This represented less than 1 percent of the nation's half a million elected posts.

Both presidents George Bush and Bill Clinton have appointed several Latino federal officials. In early 1993, the Senate confirmed Federico Peña as secretary of transportation and Henry G. Cisneros as secretary of housing and urban development (HUD). Cisneros quickly discovered that the HUD appointees of Reagan and Bush had promoted racial segregation—an attitude of "Let's just put them on the other side of the tracks and keep them there."[5]

It is probably in the field of education that Latino professionals have gained the most. Because of the establishment of bilingual programs, Spanish-speaking college graduates had some job opportunities open to them in public schools and colleges. There is now a small handful of Latino administrators in several school systems, even a few college presidents. Most of them work in majority Latino school districts, where students and their parents demanded an increase in Latino personnel. Many Latinos involved in the social movements of the sixties and seventies pioneered research in the history and culture of Latinos during their college days and later created Chicano Studies, Puerto Rican Studies, and bilingual teacher-education programs. They include prominent scholars like Rodolfo Acuña (see chapter 4), Edna Acosta-Belén (author of outstanding books on Puerto Ricans), and many others. The Reagan-Bush cutbacks in funding for research and bilingual programs have seriously damaged this important work.

For decades many highly accomplished Latino scientists and engineers migrated to the United States, attracted by the existence of advanced programs and research facilities. They are part of what is called the brain drain from the rest of the world. In recent years more have come, fleeing political turmoil in Latin America. No one questions their talents and accomplishments.

Yet Latinos raised in the United States, for all of the reasons of poverty and substandard schools outlined earlier, have "had a dismal record of entering the medical and scientific professions."[6] Those who have somehow managed to overcome the hurdles have achieved recognition as outstanding scientists in a wide variety of fields, from nuclear science to genetics. Many of them attempt to encourage young students to major in science and mathematics, knowing that what Hostos College president Isaura Santiago says is true. Santiago had planned to major in science but switched to a liberal arts major when she "found out my ghetto schooling left me unprepared for the tough competition from students from New York City's better schools."[7]

To start a new business, of course, a college degree is not a requirement. With the government's Small Business Administration granting loans to occasional Latinos, a few have been able to start their own enterprises. Most Latino businesses are small firms and stores, hiring only a few workers. It is well known that small businesses often fail but, taken altogether, they generate most of the nation's jobs and train several thousand workers who go on to work for larger companies.

Latino firms grew in number by 81 percent between 1982 and 1987. They then numbered 422,373, or 3 percent of the 12 to 13 million non-Latino firms—but only 1 percent of total gross receipts. Part of the reason is that service industries account for almost half of Latino-owned firms but earn only a quarter of total receipts. Latino businesses are usually concentrated in a few poorer areas without access to sectors of the population that spend more money.[8]

Latino small businesspeople have attitudes toward their workers similar to those of other businesspeople. In 1993, *Hispanic* magazine described their reaction to President Clinton's health plan: "Hispanic business owners worry that . . . costs would increase for many minority-owned small businesses that now pay nothing toward their workers' health insurance and would be forced to do so under Clinton's proposal."[9] The writer of the article failed to mention the desperate need for health insurance among Latinos, as well as the serious health problems affecting them.

Since there are so many newspapers, magazines, and radio and television programs in Spanish, we might expect a high degree of Latino ownership in the mass media. In fact, the opposite is true. The "big three" of Latino television—Univisión (bought by Hallmark in 1988), Galavisión, and Telemundo—are owned almost entirely by Euroamericans. Latino ownership may be rare, but it shows up significantly in smaller and specialty areas, such as the underground press of the 1960s and 1970s—alternative publications like Los Angeles' Chicano *La Raza*, Milwaukee's Latino *La Guardia*, or the Cuban Americans' pro-Cuban Revolution *Areito*. There are several high-quality Latino academic journals of use to students and teachers, including *Aztlán* and the *Bulletin of the Centro de Estudios Puertorriqueños*.

Thinking that natural talent can win success, some Latinos turn to sports, acting, and the arts. It is not so easy. Sports careers often start with athletic scholarships to colleges, rarely awarded to Latino students in barrio schools without sports teams. Furthermore, most sports require the purchase of expensive equipment, lessons, and access to special playing areas such as golf courses (usually part of exclusive country clubs) and tennis courts. Basketball, baseball, and boxing can be played with less expensive equipment on the street or in neighborhood playgrounds and gyms.

Latinos have excelled in boxing, soccer (a Latin American national pastime), and especially baseball (popular in countries bordering the Caribbean). Many of these athletes first achieve recognition in their own countries and then immigrate to the United States. In Latin America baseball never had any color lines, but in the United States in the early part of the century nonwhite Latinos were relegated to the Negro Leagues. Only light-skinned Cuban and other Latino ballplayers who could pass as white were brought into the major leagues. Probably the most famous Latino baseball player was four-time National League batting champion Roberto Clemente (1934–1972), who died in a plane crash during a mission to Nicaragua to deliver

Latinos in sports: (facing page, top) Puerto Rican Roberto Clemente, baseball Hall of Famer; (bottom) Puerto Rican Angel Cordero, three-time winner of the Kentucky Derby; and (above) Mexican-American Pancho Gonzalez, tennis champion.

relief supplies to earthquake victims. Many Puerto Rican baseball fans consider him a national hero. Latinos in major league baseball receive less money than other baseball players, although a few have become millionaires.[10]

In horse racing, Latinos excel. Puerto Rican jockey Angel Cordero, born in 1942, recently retired to become a trainer. He was a three-time Kentucky Derby winner.

A few Latinos have managed to gain access to more elitist sports. One of the most famous tennis players, Richard Alonzo "Pancho" Gonzalez (born 1928), the son of Mexican immigrants, taught himself the game at age twelve on public tennis courts in Los Angeles. From 1954 to 1962, he dominated professional tennis. Making their way into an expensive sport through "back doors," golf champions Juan (Chi) Rodriguez, born in Puerto Rico, and Lee Treviño, a Mexican American from Texas, both from poor families, worked as a caddies for wealthy players, practicing the game during time-off periods.

Many Latinos have achieved success as actors. Their distinguished acting record predates film. Latino theater flourished in nineteenth-century Florida, especially in Ybor City and the Tampa cigarmakers' Centro Obrero union headquarters. In the early barrios of New York City, Latinos performed Spanish melodramas and Cuban plays as early as 1892, in rented halls. Mutual aid societies sometimes raised funds by holding theater parties.

During the Mexican Revolution, Mexico's theater companies toured the United States, wherever there were Spanish-speaking audiences, some of them settling permanently. The works of famous Spanish playwrights were often produced, but even more popular were dramas about the struggles of Mexicans in the Southwest, written by local writers.

Variety shows gradually displaced dramatic plays in both the American and Latino theaters, but there were important differences between the two. American vaudeville emphasized slapstick comedy routines, but the Mexican *revistas* (revues), like later black, Latino, and feminist comics, used material laden with political satire, often on the theme of racism. Latino circuses and tent theaters called *carpas* also toured Latino neighborhoods, providing entertainment at lower costs than the spectacular American circuses.

In the 1930s serious playwrights performed in clubs and *mutualista* societies, but *obra bufa cubana* (Afro-Cuban revues), perhaps because of the hard times of the Depression, drew much larger audiences. The most famous of all the bufos was Arquimides Pous, whose routines were laden with savage attacks on racism. Tampa became the site of the only Latino company supported by the Federal Theater Project of the Works Progress Administration (WPA). Anglo and Latino companies shared the theater, sometimes combining forces to produce bilingual plays. In 1937, during a nativist upsurge, many foreigners were removed from the WPA and the Latino unit folded.

New York City's El Teatro Hispano opened in 1937 and became a family gathering place for almost two decades. Plays written by Cubans, Spaniards, and Puerto Ricans were performed; films were shown; and there were raffles, contests, and special performances for children. Puerto Rican theater artists founded El Nuevo Círculo Dramático in the 1950s. By 1964, theater impresario Joseph Papp's New York Shakespeare Festival was producing Shakespearean works in Spanish.

In 1965 an extraordinary theater was born when Luis Valdez created El Teatro Campesino. Valdez, a member of the well-known San Francisco Mime Troupe, left the group that year to work with the United Farm Workers. To raise money for the grape boycott and strikers' fund, he organized students and farmworkers into a company of actors dramatizing the plight of the grape pickers. The theater group of amateurs developed into a remarkable troupe of professionals, performing in film and on Broadway.

By 1970 the Chicano theater movement was in full

swing all over the country, performing plays about the farm-workers' struggle, the Vietnam War, educational struggles, and other issues of concern to Latinos. Many groups dis-banded in the 1980s as the Chicano movement that sup-ported it declined, but by then a new generation of talented Chicano and Latino playwrights had emerged. In the mid-1980s, the Ford Foundation funded Latino theater com-panies and the nation's leading Latino publishing house, Arte Público Press, to publish works by Latino writers.

In New York, improvisational street theater tradition-ally had brought politics to the streets. Although few flour-ished financially except in the 1960s, some managed to survive through private and government funding. Also dur-ing the 1960s, "Nuyorican" theater emerged, created by Puerto Ricans born and raised in New York. Miguel Piñero (1946–1988), an ex-convict who began writing in jail, won an Obie and the New York Drama Critics Best American Play Award for the 1973–1974 season for his story of jail life, *Short Eyes*, later made into a film.

Today, Latino theater flourishes in New York. Dramatists and poets read their works at the Lower East Side's Puerto Rican Poets' Café. Miami theater, where Cubans have founded several companies, produces Broadway hits in Spanish as well as classics and new plays.

Most Latinos are moviegoers. As films became more popular and profitable after World War II, attendance at live performances dwindled and most theaters were con-verted into movie houses. From the earliest days of the film industry, Latino performers faced serious barriers in Hollywood. For one thing, films were costly to make, and producers aimed their films at larger Euroamerican audi-ences, catering to all of their preferences and prejudices. Latino performers had two choices: take stereotyped parts or earn their living in some other way.

The stereotypes were far worse than the "sleepy Mexican" theme still appearing in modern films. "The early cinematic depiction of the Hispanic was an almost unrelieved exercise in degradation," one expert commentator flatly states.[11] The word greaser was a common part of film titles like *The Greaser's Gauntlet*, produced by D. W. Griffith. Other Latino types were equally insulting—the bandido (bandit), buffoon, dark lady, and gay caballero. Anglo actors pursued vile and vicious *bandidos*, roared over the foolishness of Mexican buffoons, and seduced Spanish dancers (dark ladies) of questionable morals (but seldom married them!). Lupe Vélez, particularly popular with Mexican audiences, received star billing as "The Mexican Spitfire." The gay caballero, a charming but oversexed Latino hero, was also a box office hit. The Cisco Kid character was the best-known version, with Cesar Romero often playing the role.

Latinos who could "pass" for Anglo often changed their names in order to escape the stereotyped roles. Margarita Carmen Cansino was transformed into Rita Hayworth. Likewise, Raquel Tejada became love goddess Raquel Welch.

During the 1930s Depression the situation for African American and Latino actors improved. Social problem films attempted to rectify the past racial slurs. To increase box office receipts, however, well-known Anglo actors in dark makeup were often hired to play Latino parts. Paul Muni, for example, appeared in brownface as Johnny Ramirez in *Bordertown*, and as late as 1979, Robby Benson wore brown contact lenses to play a Latino in *Walk Proud*. But a few Latino actors, such as Ricardo Montalbán and Anthony Quinn, were able to embark on careers without "passing" (although often in grade B movies or supporting roles).

During the Cold War witch-hunt period, many of the writers and directors of social problem films were black-listed. Social problems were considered off-limits for film fare, and stereotypes of Latinos in Westerns were revived. *Salt of the Earth* (1954), the "first feature film ever made in this country of labor, by labor, and for labor,"[12] and *The Lawless* (1950), an outspoken film about racism against Chicanos, were both written by blacklisted Hollywood script writers and were banned from most theaters due to the power of the film studio heads.

The situation changed later, for both financial and political reasons. In the late 1950s, trade journals commented on the growth of the black filmgoing population, suggesting that there would be a profitable market for films appealing to African Americans. Sidney Poitier's extraordinary box office success convinced many filmmakers. As the witch-hunt declined and the civil rights movement grew, suits were threatened to force the film industry to hire minorities. At first, African-American actors were hired to play bit parts usually reserved for whites and then went on to produce many "blaxploitation—superspade" (sterotypical and exploitative of blacks) films.

The film industry was not convinced that Latinos were an important enough audience and were under less pressure from them at first. Portrayals of Latinos in films were either nonexistent or reverted back to more sophisticated versions of the same old stereotypes. For example, with the days of strict censorship on nudity and sex behind them, Hollywood dusted off the gay caballero, making him an insatiable, hot-blooded Latin lover.

In the late 1960s, the Latino community and civil rights groups like LULAC and MALDEF campaigned against offensive television characters used in commercials like Frito Bandito and Chiquita Banana and the lack of Latino representation in the film industry. Latino actors and media workers also organized, demanding a better image and more roles in films. Latino characters played by Latinos began to appear in films like *West Side Story* in 1961, with Rita Moreno in a major role, but these films were the exception. In 1969, the EEOC pointed out that only 3 percent of the workforce at Hollywood studios was "Spanish surnamed."

Matters slowly improved, but Chicanos, believing that only their own films would tell the full truth, developed a new Chicano documentary cinema. Luis and Daniel Valdez of El Teatro Campesino produced one of the first Chicano films, the 1967 adaptation of Rodolfo "Corky" Gonzales's epic poem *I Am Joaquín*. Dozens of films were produced reenacting historic events like the Delano grape strike as well as portraying Latinos' daily lives. Most of them were shown in small art theaters and on public television.

Television networks hired a few Latino actors to play ongoing roles in series. Puerto Rican comedian Freddy Prinze, already a proven star attraction, was given a vehicle of his own (*Chico and the Man*). Latinos with regular parts usually bore nonethnic names and had light skin, like Victoria Principal of *Dallas*. More often, in films about Latinos, like the story of a Puerto Rican father, *Popi*, the title role was played not by one of the many unemployed Latino actors but by Alan Arkin! The talented Martin Sheen (Estevez) enjoyed a notable acting career from the late 1960s to the present.

As protest against this barring of Latinos from the media heightened and Latinos became the second largest minority group in the United States, there were profound changes. Tired of waiting for major film companies to change their policies, Moctezuma Esparza coestablished Esparza/Katz productions and raised money for films on Latino themes. Successful actors like Edward James Olmos and Andy Garcia also became film producers.

Public television (PBS) began producing more Latino works, including documentaries like *Los Mineros* (The Miners, 1991).

As the Latino market broadened, a phenomena called "Hispanic Hollywood" emerged. Several films on Latino themes were released in the late 1980s on the Chicano experience—from *La Bamba* on Mexican-American rock music star Richie Valens to *Stand and Deliver*, a social protest type film on the education of Latinos. Films made in and about Latin America did well. *El Norte*, a movie about two young refugees from political repression in Guatemala, received rave reviews and was seen by millions.

Comic team "Cheech" Marin and Thomas Chong were big box office hits as Cheech and Chong. Several new box office stars emerged, like Rachel Ticotin, Martin Sheen's sons Charlie Sheen and Emilio Estevez, and others.

Latino comics appeared on national television. Colombia-born Obie winner John Leguizamo, "the Mambo Mouth," displayed a wit similar to the funny men of the old Mexican *revistas*. Accused of creating stereotypes, he commented, "I take them and turn them around. It's like getting those demons out there and hitting them over the head." Raised in Queens, Leguizamo says that his critics tend to be what he calls "the Hispanic bourgeoisie, who hate portrayals of Latinos that do not conform to their view of themselves."[13]

Just as the situation seemed finally to be improving for Latino performers, their progress was endangered by the deteriorating economy of the 1990s. "It's more difficult now than ever before," says Ray Blanco, president of the national Hispanic Academy for Media and Arts and Sciences. "They are taking fewer chances with unknown actors."[14]

Latino writers did not face the same problems of visible skin color faced by performers, but publishers' fears of an inadequate Latino book-buying public were impediments to success. Although a few prominent authors like Mexico's Carlos Fuentes or Colombia's Nobel Prize laureate Gabriel García Márquez had their works translated into English, newer writers faced great difficulties. An awakening interest in Latinos and the emergence of a Latino middle class improved the situation. The best known work by a Latino is still Piri Thomas's heart-wrenching *Down These Mean Streets* (1967) in which he sets down on paper his gut feelings about growing up black, poor, and Puerto Rican in the 1950s.

Richard Rodriguez's 1982 award-winning autobiography *Hunger of Memory* reveals the devastating impact on darker-skinned Latinos of the racism of white society against black people. It leads to too many Latinos denying their own racial heritage, even "whitening" their appearance and attitudes in order to get ahead. Rodríguez poignantly describes how he tried to shave off his dark skin with a razor blade when he was a youth. He explains how he had to surrender his Mexican-American heritage to "make it" in the white world. Yet the price he paid was very high: he felt emotionally dead inside because he no longer had the warmth, love, and friendliness of his "Mexican" family. Rodríguez was criticized by other Latinos for his condemnation of affirmative action, which he claims perpetuated "the creation of an elite society": "Activists pushed to get more nonwhite students into colleges. . . . The revolutionary demand would have called for a reform of primary and secondary schools."[15] Many activists countered that they did call for reforms at *all* levels of education, but the results were far from satisfactory.

Many other Latino writers have gained recognition for their excellence. In 1990, novelist Oscar Hijuelos, the son of Cuban- American working-class parents in New York City, became the first Latino to win the Pulitzer Prize for Fiction (*The Mambo Kings Play Songs of Love*). Nicholasa Mohr, raised in Spanish Harlem and, like Hijuelos, educated in New York City schools, is one of the very few Latinas who have managed to achieve national recognition as creative writers.

During the upsurge in Latino protest movements in the 1960s and early 1970s, a veritable renaissance in Latino art occurred. Finding themselves locked out of the official art world by gallery owners, museum directors, and art critics, Latinos created their own art galleries from coast to coast.

Drawing on the examples of Mexico's great muralists, Chicano artists in the United States began creating their own unique mural art speaking to cultural pride, and the needs of the poor and calling for an end to the Vietnam War. Their street murals—and those of other Latinos—

*Cuban-American novelist
Oscar Hijuelos, Pulitzer Prize winner*

were so original and powerful that they superseded the Mexicans of the 1920s and 1930s as the driving force of contemporary mural art in the 1970s. Their most original contribution was in linking their art directly to people's struggles—creating a people's art. Several of the more successful Latino muralists went on to gain national and international recognition.

Many Latino muralists and some other prominent Latino artists have been more concerned about the future of Latino youth than about their own careers. Orlando Agudelo-Botero tours his art show "Luz—Education Through Art" to barrio schools, introducing children, many for the first time, to the world of art. "I would like to bring light to someone else's life," he explains.[16]

Just as many Latino actors and artists have had to make their living precariously in street theater and art, many talented musicians have had to do the same thing. Some, such as the still "undiscovered" ageless street singer Lares, a Puerto Rican woman farmworker, have entertained the homeless and migrant communities for decades.[17]

The contributions of Latinos to the world of music are legendary. Who has not danced—or wanted to dance—to the Argentine tango, Colombian cumbia, Dominican merengue, Cuban rumba, Mexican mariachi, Chicanos' La Onda Chicano (Chicano Wave), or Caribbean salsa? These and other original Latino musical forms have a long history rooted in Spanish and African traditions and the struggles of Latin America's working class.

Latinos also have made major contributions to classical music and jazz. Lack of financial resources, however, has limited the number of successful Latino classical musicians, dancers, and singers. The handful of success stories, like cellist Pablo Casals or pianist Claudio Arrau, almost always come from well-off families in Spain or Latin America. Casals, considered the greatest cellist of all time, adopted Puerto Rico as his home rather than live in fascist Spain under the dictator, General Franco.[18] Dancer and choreographer Tina Ramirez, of Mexican-Puerto Rican heritage, founded New York's Ballet Hispánico in 1970, noted for its mix of modern and classical styles. Puerto Rican Julia Migenes-Johnson made it all the way to New York's Metropolitan Opera.

There is a rich Latino heritage of folk, jazz, and popular music that places Latinos alongside blacks as major creators of American music. The Mexican-American vocal *corrido* (ballad) and ensemble *conjunto/orquesta* traditions of Texas are world renowned. In the 1920s and 1930s, the *conjunto/orquesta* began to blend with the American and Caribbean jazz movements but never lost their original Mexican sound.

Generations of African-American, African-Cuban, and Latino jazz musicians have enriched one another's creations. For example, in the late 1930s the traditional Cuban folk form known as the *son* was transformed into the "big band sound" of jazz musicians like Count Basie, Duke Ellington, and Stan Kenton. Clarinetist Alcide "Yellow" Nuñez formed the Original Dixieland Jazz Band, giving rise to that unique form. Many other Latinos have gone on to compose, perform, and star in the nation's jazz clubs. Finally, there is the recent Latino jazz/rock movement of musicians like Chick Corea and Carlos Santana. It carries on the Latinos' multicultural musical tradition with strong Caribbean rhythms and innovations.

Salsa (sauce) too has deep roots in Afro-Caribbean musical and religious traditions. Its adaptation of American jazz's horn sounds has made it even more multicultural today. While much of salsa has become commercialized, it has not lost touch with its antislavery and social protest roots. The 1983 hit by Ruben Blades quoted at the start of this chapter is similar to themes in his other songs: Latinos are important for "freeing" America from conformity and materialism.[19]

As in all other groups, of course, only a small minority of Latinos have special talents for the sciences and arts.

The vast majority want a decent job that makes it possible for them to have a better life. Unfortunately, Latinos are still largely excluded from better-paying jobs. Federally funded job training and affirmative action programs have been all but eliminated, despite the fact that a 1985 U.S. Department of Labor study revealed that, for each dollar invested, the short-lived federal Job Corps program returned $1.38 in the form of taxes paid by former trainees as well as reduced welfare payments. In top management positions in large corporations, at least 96 percent of the positions are still held by white males. In better-paying fields like construction, progress has also been reversed in most states.[20]

The impact of civil rights legislation on Latinos' job opportunities was also severely weakened by Supreme Court decisions when the majority of justices were appointed by Presidents Reagan and Bush. The right to sue under the 1964 Civil Rights Act, for example, was severely undermined by several legal decisions. Representatives of civil rights organizations attempted to pass a new Civil Rights Act in 1990, restoring some of the gains of the old laws. Both houses of Congress supported the bill, but the Bush administration vetoed it.

Virginia Ruiz, an officer of the Asociación Nacional México-Americana (ANMA, 1949–1954), once proclaimed that for Latinos to win their fight for equal rights they would have "to have the closest unity with our strongest ally, the Negro people."[21] Attempts at building that unity had come and gone, usually during workers' strikes (see chapter 3). In recent decades, unity between minority groups has helped stem the tide of budgetary rollbacks, but with each group scrambling to survive there have been all too few joint efforts.

The media has labeled the economic changes of recent hard times the restructuring of the economy, which means in reality that employers are looking for cheaper labor in order to "become more competitive" with (make more profits than) Japan, Europe, and one another. That translates into lower living standards for most Americans and increased poverty for those already poor.

Since 1973, a majority of Americans have indeed been getting poorer, their wages able to buy less than before. Poverty rates in the good year 1987 were higher than even the bad recession year of 1980. The gap between rich and poor widened during those years, as the incomes of the poorest fifth of the population dropped by 10 percent while those of the wealthiest fifth grew by 16 percent.[22] As the job market proceeds to create a few good (well-paid) jobs and a lot of bad (poorly paid) ones, Latinos fall even further behind.

Some do better than others. Among Latinos as a group, Cubans and South Americans stand at the top of the income pyramid, Central Americans in the middle, and Mexicans and Puerto Ricans at the bottom. But there are significant numbers of poor people in every national sub-group in the nation, including Cubans.[23]

Today one of every four Latino families lives in poverty—three times the number of white families. Per person, non-Cuban Latinos have barely half the income of Cuban Americans and non-Latinos. The 1990 census found 38.4 percent of Latino children living in poverty. The *lowest* estimate of the number of America's children going to bed hungry every night is a shocking 12 million—many are Latinos.[24]

Even when Latinos are able to find work, they often fill the ranks of the working poor—those employed but at such low wages that they fall below the poverty line.[25] Perhaps most shocking is the level of poverty among Puerto Ricans, the nation's worst-off group. In 1990 Puerto Ricans' poverty level stood at 40.6 percent, compared with African Americans' 31.9 percent, all Latinos' 28.1 percent, and whites' 10.7 percent.[26] A horrifying 56.7 percent of Puerto Rican children are being raised in poverty. There are two reasons for the Puerto Ricans' deteriorating situation.

Thirty-nine percent of Puerto Rican families are headed by a female, compared with a national figure of 16.5 percent and a Mexican and Mexican-American figure of 19 percent. Women in the United States, on average, continue to receive less than 60 percent of the wage of males in equivalent work. Obviously, women supporting families on their own often fall below the poverty line. To make matters worse, the industries in which Puerto Rican women traditionally worked, such as garment manufacturing, are more often circumventing union wages by hiring newly arrived nonunionized workers from the Dominican Republic, Colombia, and other countries and paying them less.[27]

Whether for Puerto Ricans, Dominicans, or most other Latinos, male or female, the trend is clear: more poverty and inequality. The old upward mobility myth of success just doesn't work for the vast majority of today's immigrants, any more than it did for yesterday's.[28] As the educational and skill levels required to get a job increase and as most Latinos face low-paying, dead-end jobs, the existing income gap widens not only between Latinos and non-Latinos but also between the handful of Latinos who "make it" and the majority of Latinos who do not.

As we will discover in the next chapter, even as Latinos continue to fight for a place in the sun in the world of higher education and professional jobs, they are also fighting for economic equity in the workforce as a whole, an indispensable component of a democratic nation.

6
seis

GUARANTEEING

OUR

RIGHTS

Not like the brazen giant of Greek fame,
With conquering limbs astride from land to land:
Here at our sea-washed, sunset gates shall stand
A mighty woman with a torch, whose flame
Is the imprisoned lightning, and her name
Mother of Exiles. From her beacon-hand
Glows world-wide welcome: her mild eyes command
The air-bridged harbor that twin cities frame.
"Keep, ancient lands, your storied pomp!" cries she
With silent lips. Give me your tired, your poor,
Your huddled masses yearning to breathe free,
The wretched refuse of your teeming shore.
Send these, the homeless, tempest-tossed, to me,
I lift my lamp beside the golden door!
      —Emma Lazarus's verse on the Statue of Liberty[1]

When one describes the best that America offers, many think of words like freedom, democracy, and equality and a chance to gain some economic well-being and happiness in life. Usually political democracy is emphasized. The national anthem ends with the words "the land of the free and the home of the brave." The Statue of Liberty contrasts the United States with ancient imperialism, "the brazen giant of Greek fame." With its torch of freedom it beckons "huddled masses yearning to breathe free" to enter through a "golden door" of new chances in life.

But without *economic* democracy—freedom from poverty—political freedom becomes less important. The economic aspect of liberty usually went unmentioned until January 6, 1941, when President Franklin Delano Roosevelt placed it among the "four essential freedoms" in his annual State-of-the-Union message. Along with the well-known political freedoms of speech and religion, he added an economic right, "freedom from want."[2]

Clearly, democracy—both political and economic—is the bedrock of the American Dream. The Constitution's first ten amendments, known as the Bill of Rights, define the fundamental liberties, human rights. The most important ones are: freedom of religion, speech, press, assembly, and petition (First Amendment); prohibition of unreasonable searches and seizure (Fourth); no taking of life, liberty, or property without "due process of law" (Fifth); the right to a speedy trial by "an impartial jury" and the right to legal counsel (Sixth); and prohibitions against excessive bail or cruel and unusual punishment (Eighth).

Political democracy is often thought to be a democratically elected government that guarantees these inalienable rights, one that derives, in the words of the U.S. Declaration of Independence, its "just powers from the consent of the governed." People give their consent when they vote in "free elections," where *everyone* of voting age is supposed to have an *equal* chance to vote. So valuable are these basic rights that the Declaration of Independence affirms "that whenever any Form of Government becomes destructive of these ends, it is the Right of the People to alter or abolish it."

But all know that lofty declarations are not the law. Most later constitutional amendments, viewed as adding to the Bill of Rights, were won after long and sometimes bloody struggles. The Thirteenth, Fourteenth, and Fifteenth amendments abolished slavery and gave the newly freed African Americans guarantees that were to apply to all Americans—the right to a fair trial (due process), equal protection of the laws, and the right to vote regardless of race.

Of course the Bill of Rights did not spell out the specifics of all these guarantees. Words like "free speech," "due process," and "equal protection" can be vague, and throughout American history all men and women have *not* been treated as though they were "created equal." For years, Latino and African-American children were segregated in inferior schools, by law (de jure segregation) in the South and by impoverished ghettoes that created segregated housing (de facto segregation) in other parts of the nation. Many people wondered if equal education and job opportunities weren't part of the promise of the Bill of Rights.

And what about "due process"? When juries were chosen, they were usually all-white. In the 1992 Rodney King case in which Los Angeles police officers beat and injured African-American Rodney King, the predominantly white jury acquitted the police.

Many Latinos realize that guarantees on paper mean little if they aren't reflected in everyday life. Latinos and their organizations are prominent among this nation's defenders of political and economic democracy. Yet their significant contributions are rarely recognized.

In the nineteenth century, most Latinos identified with three democratic causes: abolition of slavery, labor's rights, and an end to Spanish colonialism. In New York City, Cuban and Puerto Rican immigrants supported exiles from the Dominican Republic in the victorious struggle for that nation's "Second Independence" (1865), led by African-Dominican Gregorio Luperón. They also formed the anti-slavery Republican Society of Cuba and Puerto Rico.

The leader of the struggle for Cuban independence from Spain, poet José Martí, lived most of his adult life in New York City (1881–1895). He wrote insightful articles for important local newspapers and national magazines on the flaws in American democracy and on the early labor movement's attempts to correct them. Cuban tobacco workers in Florida joined Martí's revolutionary party in droves. An outspoken critic of racism, Martí opposed early attempts by the United States to run Latin America's affairs. He died in Cuba in a battle against Spanish troops, believing that "the Cuban war has broken out in time to prevent the annexation of Cuba to the United States."[3]

After the Spanish-Cuban-American War, the United States became the dominant economic power in Latin America. In the name of defending freedom and protecting U.S. investments (called "dollar diplomacy," and also known as "gunboat diplomacy"), U.S. Marines invaded almost all the countries of the Caribbean and Central America. The marines put down an African-Cuban uprising in 1912 and subsequent attempts to free the island of Cuba from U.S.-backed dictators. In 1933, the United States refused to recognize the Cuban leader of another attempted revolution and supported a new dictator, Fulgencio Batista, who ruled until the Cuban Revolution of 1959 led by Fidel Castro.

As citizens, Puerto Ricans have always had an easier time than other Latin Americans entering the United States. Up until the 1940s, most mainland Puerto Ricans supported democracy by backing the labor movement here and independence for the island "back home." When New York City's El Barrio rallied to Congressman Vito Marcantonio (see chapter 3), one reason was that he loudly protested the jailing of Nationalist Party leader Pedro Albizu Campos and the U.S. military's 1937 Ponce Massacre.[4]

*José Martí, leader of the
Cuban nationalist movement*

Before the Civil War, Mexicans residing in northern Mexico (today's Texas and American Southwest) predating annexation by the United States were sympathetic to the plight of American slaves. When their government abolished slavery in 1829, some of the Mexicans helped runaway slaves from the southern states and the disputed territory, called by American settlers the "Republic of Texas," to find safety in Mexico. After the 1846–1848 U.S.-Mexico War, Mexicans and Native Americans in the Southwest were stripped of 20 million acres of land by Euroamerican settlers. Victimized by rapes, lynchings, and land thefts, Mexican people rebelled, demanding their rights. Social bandits—heroes like Texas's Juan "Cheno" Cortina—carried out retaliatory raids.

During the Mexican people's fight to overthrow the Díaz dictatorship of 1876–1911, Mexican Americans rallied to the PLM (see chapter 3). Its pro-democracy program of 1906 called for the protection of Mexican immigrants' human rights in the United States. PLM organizers also played a central role in the fight for economic democracy—"freedom from want"—helping to organize labor unions and strikes in both countries.

As soldiers and workers, Latinos played a key role in saving American democracy during both world wars. Puerto Ricans, as we learned in chapter 3, were made citizens in order to make them eligible to fight in Europe's trenches during World War I. Latinos, including Mexicans imported to make up for the labor shortage, kept the mines and railroads operating during both world conflagrations. Latina women entered the copper mines to keep production going for the World War II effort. They and 68,000 specially imported Mexican braceros (see chapter 1) also kept the nation's railroads running. Braceros and Mexican-American families produced most of the food that fed the troops. Latinos received more Medals of Honor than any other group fighting in World War II.[5]

Despite these vital contributions, Latinos suffered from

renewed outbursts of racism, like 1943's "zoot suit" riots (see chapter 3). To fight for democracy at home and not just overseas, the Spanish-Speaking People's Congress—*El Congreso*—formed an alliance with the Jewish People's Committee and the NAACP to launch the Council for the Protection of Minority Rights. Its efforts led to the creation of the federal Fair Employment Practices Committee (FEPC) in 1941 to monitor discrimination by private companies with government contracts. Although largely ineffective and terminated after the war years, the FEPC was an important precursor of today's EEOC (Equal Employment Opportunity Commission).

Latinos have a long record of trying to improve the criminal justice system. They have often been the victims of injustice at the hands of the nation's lawmen, assigned to protect them from racist violence. In 1942, El Congreso's Josefina Fierro de Bright and others formed the Sleepy Lagoon Defense Committee in Los Angeles. Nine Mexican-American youths had been falsely accused and convicted of second-degree murder charges in an affair having to do with police vengeance against Los Angeles' "38th Street Club." The FBI branded the defense committee's members as "un-American," but thanks to the committee's efforts, an appeals court two years later reversed the youths' conviction for lack of evidence. FBI harassment, however, forced *El Congreso* to dissolve before the final victory.

After the war, Latinos and African Americans, often with the help of Jewish Americans, continued to play a leading role in the battle to make the promise of juridical and political democracy a reality. Besides the well-known Supreme Court decision on desegregating the public schools in 1954, an extremely important case about jury selection came before the Court that same year.

Pete Hernández had been convicted of the murder of Joe Espinosa by an all-white jury in Jackson County, Texas (18 percent Latino). In *Hernández* v. *Texas*, LULAC lawyer Gus García argued that even if Hernández was guilty it was a clear-cut case of discrimination in jury selection, since Mexican Americans were treated "as a class apart"—a violation of the Fourteenth Amendment's "equal protection" clause. Agreeing with García, the Supreme Court censured Jackson County for not allowing a single Mexican American to serve on a jury in twenty-five years.[6] Despite that court decision, *as late as the mid-1970s* an Anglo lawyer in Dallas said that in a dozen years of practice "he had never seen an Hispanic on a jury."[7]

Political democracy almost perished during the Cold War in the "silent fifties," when most Americans were afraid to exercise their free speech rights. Some who spoke out were fired from their jobs and had great difficulty finding others. Civil rights organizations moved cautiously in order to avoid the inquisitors of the House Un-American Activities Committee. LULAC managed to stay out of trouble by moving into the electoral arena, backing conservative Mexican-American air force veteran Raymond Telles, elected mayor of El Paso in 1957. Prior to the civil rights movement, LULAC won only occasional victories that desegregated neighborhood restaurants or movie theaters that had excluded Latinos.[8]

The *only* civil rights organization in the nation to denounce the witch-hunt's curtailment of the precious freedoms guaranteed by the Bill of Rights was a Latino one: the *Asociación Nacional México-Americana* (ANMA—National Mexico-American Association). It took considerable courage for ANMA to expose publicly the many violations of civil liberties during the heyday of McCarthyism. It campaigned vigorously, for example, against worker firings and deportations authorized by the 1950 and 1952 McCarran-Walter Immigration Acts. ANMA also campaigned against Operation Wetback at the very time ANMA was being hounded out of existence by the FBI. Despite its brief life, ANMA is now well recognized for its heroic defense of democracy during the darkest days of McCarthyism.

President Truman had vetoed the 1950 McCarran-Walter Act, considering it unconstitutional, but Congress overrode his veto. Under the law's provisions, naturalized Americans could have their citizenship revoked. The Act mandated the construction of "emergency" concentration camps. Six of the camps were built by 1952—an early precedent for the type of detention centers that were overflowing with unwanted immigrants and political refugees from Central America and Haiti in the nineties.

For decades the McCarran-Walter Acts slammed "the golden door" on *anyone* suspected of sympathizing with communism. Among those excluded were Nobel Prize winners like Colombian novelist Gabriel García Márquez, as well as 3,000 Canadians, among them mainstream trade unionists and politicians. The Acts were also used to justify Operation Wetback and other efforts to intimidate immigrant workers, smash labor unions, and harass the nation's Latino minority.[9]

In the 1940s and 1950s, new Latino civil rights groups emerged. Besides ANMA, two stood out: the American GI Forum and the Community Service Organization (CSO). World War II veterans like thirty-three-year-old Bronze Star winner Army Medical Corpsman Héctor Pérez García founded the GI Forum in 1947 after Texas cemeteries refused to handle the body of a Mexican-American soldier killed in combat. A popular *corrido* of the time lamented: "Not even in a cemetery do they admit a Mexican."[10] The GI Forum is still active today and lobbies for Latino civil rights.

The CSO advocated nonviolent mass action and bloc voting in elections. One of its first directors was farmworker leader Cesar Chavez. The CSO helped organize southern California's Civic Unity Leagues, whose Latina women played leading roles in voter registration drives. As a result, Edward R. Roybal was elected to the Los Angeles City Council in 1949, the first councilman of Mexican descent since 1881—a small step forward for political democracy.

Puerto Ricans also kept up their struggle for full democratic rights. After the end of World War II, their homeland won the right to have its own governor. In 1952 Puerto Rico was given commonwealth status after a referendum on the question offered no independence option. Today, the United Nations and Puerto Rico's political parties acknowledge the island is a colony.

By 1950 there were 63,000 registered Puerto Rican voters in Congressman Marcantonio's district of El Barrio, despite difficult literacy tests in English to qualify them for voting rights. Volunteers, many of them Jewish, helped Spanish Harlem's residents prepare for the tests. They kept reelecting Marcantonio. "Puerto Rico's congressman," as he was known, finally lost an election because of a redistricting maneuver in 1950. His district was redrawn to take in the "silk stocking" voters of Manhattan's posh Upper East Side. Commented two Puerto Ricans after his death in 1954: "People said he was a communist . . . but he was the best New York ever had."[11]

As the postwar witch-hunt died down, the struggle for political freedom was reinvigorated. In 1961, Puerto Ricans in New York's El Barrio rallied to a reform Democrat who opposed the corrupt party bosses. He was a Jewish American, State Assemblyman Mark Lane, who headed the East Harlem Reform Democratic Club. The club's volunteers helped elect Carlos Ríos the first Puerto Rican district leader in the city's history. Ríos won the votes of El Barrio because he campaigned for improvements in the district's rundown schools where children who spoke only Spanish had little chance of advancing.[12]

By 1960, Chicago had 30,000 Puerto Ricans, most of them living in slums. The Catholic Church–sponsored Caballeros de San Juan, which spoke out for civil rights, although the Church continued to discourage Latinos from becoming "political."[13]

The fight for economic democracy had lagged behind the struggles for political democracy. As many white

*Congressional representative of New York's El Barrio,
Vito Marcantonio (left) with two other New York City
congressmen, Adam Clayton Powell (center) and
Franklin D. Roosevelt, Jr. The three supported the
1950 Fair Employment Practices bill.*

Americans moved into suburbs and enjoyed increased affluence during the 1950s and early 1960s, African Americans, Latinos, and poor whites resented the fact that they had so little share in the pie. President Johnson's antipoverty campaign was too little too late. Short of entering the dangerous and deadly world of drug trafficking, the only way some people had to survive was to apply for welfare—a humiliating procedure. To qualify, a person had to prove there was no breadwinner living at home. This caused many irregularly employed husbands to move out, further eroding their self-confidence, already shaken by discrimination on the job market. Poor people's families, including traditionally close-knit Latino ones, were being broken up by harsh economic realities.

During the 1960s and early 1970s, even the poorest of the poor fought back. Puerto Rican and other Latina women joined the National Welfare Rights Organization (NWRO). Because of its efforts, the women won a ban against social workers appearing unannounced at clients' homes to make sure they had not bought anything new. NWRO won a federal legal aid program for those unable to afford legal assistance. It also helped extend coverage to needy immigrants—a 1971 Supreme Court decision assured resident aliens of equal access to welfare programs.[14]

As urban protests increased, police tempers grew short. Police violence triggered devastating riots and rebellions. The first Latino urban uprising, the 1966 Division Street Riot in Chicago, took place after a policeman shot a young Puerto Rican man. One Puerto Rican bystander told a reporter: "Tell the police we are not supposed to be beaten up like animals. . . . We are human beings."[15] The National Advisory Commission on Civil Disorders investigating urban revolts found white racism "essentially responsible." The Commission warned that the nation was "moving toward two societies, one black, one white—separate and unequal." It affirmed that so long as the *economic causes* of poverty and racial hatred existed, there would be riots.[16]

Little changed. President Johnson said that the government could finance the Vietnam War *and* end poverty—"guns and butter," he claimed. But the war soon drained the antipoverty budget and poor people continued to live poorly, with neither much butter nor the luxurious food that better-off Americans ate.

Latinos also saw their sons go off to fight in Vietnam in far greater numbers than young white men. Before the antiwar movement won its demand for a lottery draft, college students received student deferments. Few Latinos could afford college. Some, jobless and hopeless, enlisted in the army to assure themselves of three meals a day. But the Vietnam War was the nation's longest—and only losing—war. Latinos accounted for 19 percent of U.S. casualties, four times their percentage in the general population.[17]

Naturally, Latinos joined the antiwar movement's protest marches. They read the pamphlets handed out by protest organizers and learned that the United States had broken its promise to allow Vietnam to hold free elections in 1956. Instead the United States armed and defended a tyrannical dictatorship ruling South Vietnam. President Eisenhower and others had realized that the popular communist leader of the guerrillas who had thrown out the French colonialists earlier in the 1950s would easily win the election.

In Vietnam, young soldiers saw for themselves that the majority of the people of South Vietnam had little affection for the repressive South Vietnam government. When the soldiers returned home from the war, some of them in wheelchairs, some told of atrocities they had been ordered to commit against entire village populations suspected of "harboring communists." These soldiers formed the Vietnam Veterans Against the War. One of its leaders was portrayed by actor Tom Cruise in the 1989 movie *Born on the Fourth of July*, nominated for an Academy Award.

Marches of a million people and more called for an end to the "illegal [because Congress had never declared war], unjust, and immoral war." Knowing that he stood a good chance of losing reelection in 1968 because of the unpopular war (and perhaps unwilling to prosecute it), President Johnson decided not to run. The Republican candidate, Richard Nixon, campaigned on a promise to bring the troops home.

The question of who would be a candidate for the presidency had little impact on the poor. In the spring of that year, some 50,000 people set up the Poor People's Encampment in Washington, D.C., to demand either jobs or a guaranteed annual income for everyone. Dr. Martin Luther King, Jr., had helped plan the event, but he died shortly before it took place. For years he never tired of explaining why political rights, so difficult to achieve, were easier to win than economic justice. Civil rights laws came free of charge, King said. Eliminating poverty would take billions of dollars. The necessary funds were never committed.

Thousands of Latinos joined the Encampment. From out West, a Chicano contingent arrived. Men, women, and children set up tents and built wooden shacks. Despite rain, mud, and the government's failure to address their demands, they held out for weeks. One Latina later recalled proudly: "I was eight and a half months pregnant at the time and damn if I didn't go into labor. No way was I going to leave the Encampment though. I gave birth to my daughter right there. Got better treatment than I'd get at the barrio hospital!"[18]

Efforts at joint multiracial actions like the Poor People's Encampment were short-lived. Outstanding leaders who called for unity were assassinated: Malcolm X after he announced that he was willing to work with antiracist white groups; Dr. King after he linked the civil rights movement with the antiwar movement; Senator Robert Kennedy after he gained overwhelming support among Latino and African-American voters in Democratic primary elections. Two less well known and much younger leaders, Fred Hampton and

Mark Clark, Black Panthers who built the 1960s' rainbow coalition with the Young Lords and Young Patriots (see chapter 4), were framed by undercover FBI agents and murdered by Chicago police in a predawn raid on their apartment.[19]

Richard Nixon won the 1968 election but failed to carry out his promise to end the Vietnam War. The antiwar movement grew, as many more European Americans, African Americans, and Latinos joined its ranks. In 1968, an African-American contingent gathered in Harlem and then joined the massive downtown demonstration. Their signs read: "No Vietnamese Ever Called Me Nigger."

In May 1970, the National Guard killings of several white student protestors at Kent State and of black students at Jackson State, combined with Nixon's escalation of the "secret war" in Cambodia and Laos, touched off a national student strike. Mexican Americans organized a Chicano Moratorium against the war in 1970. As tens of thousands marched through Los Angeles, police violently assaulted families picnicking at the rally site. Three people were killed and hundreds more injured. One of the dead was local television news reporter Rubén Salazar, known for his TV reports on police brutality against Latinos. No one stood trial for these crimes.[20]

But the antiwar movement won an enormous victory when Nixon resigned rather than face impeachment in 1973 and the war ended in 1975. The anticolonialist communists and the majority of Vietnam's people finally achieved the unification of their country denied them by Eisenhower in 1956.

During the 1960s and 1970s, African Americans, Latinos, and others also mobilized to make democracy's voting rights work for them and not just European Americans. They won progressively democratic Voting Rights Acts. African Americans showed the way with the 1965 act eliminating the poll tax. Latinos applied pressures of their own to expand voting rights. They helped win the

1970 act banning the kind of redistricting used against Marcantonio and the 1975 act *permanently* outlawing literacy tests and requiring bilingual ballots in districts with more than 5 percent non-English-speaking voters. Finally, the 1982 Voting Rights Act prohibited state or local restrictions of access to the ballot on account of race, color, or language minority status. As a result, Latinos, Asians, Arabs, and other underrepresented Americans improved their chances for an equal voice in the electoral arena—a huge step forward for political democracy.

Those victories were dampened when shocked Americans learned about the methods used by both the Johnson and Nixon presidencies in their efforts to stem antiwar sentiment as well as voting rights activities. The Watergate scandal that helped bring about Nixon's resignation led to startling revelations on how the Bill of Rights had been scrapped.[21]

Under the cloak of national security secrecy, the Nixon administration had disregarded America's most cherished rights of democracy during those times. Repressive measures reminiscent of the persecution of immigrants and trade unionists after 1917 or during the McCarthy era were introduced.[22] The antiwar demonstrations had so incensed Nixon and Johnson that their administrations launched an all-out war on basic freedoms.

The government's COINTELPRO (Counter Intelligence Program) infiltrated and divided Latino and other activist organizations. Both the Young Lords and the Brown Berets disbanded because of so many police informants within their ranks.[23] Anyone daring to exercise their free speech rights faced harassment. Congressmen, executives of the mass media, journalists, even famous athletes and movie stars were targeted by Nixon strategists for Internal Revenue Service audits, telephone tapping, and a now honored place on Nixon's famous enemies list.

Grand juries indicted scores of activists for exercising

their right of free speech. Among those targeted were supporters of Puerto Rican independence. The friend of Albizu Campos, Carlos Feliciano, was framed on terrorist bombing charges and acquitted by an incredulous jury. Police forces formed Red Squads to hound advocates of change.

The U.S. Commission on Civil Rights later documented several beatings, shootings, and murders of Latinos. Occasional lawsuits against the authorities' illegal actions were won many years later, including one brought by the families of Black Panthers Fred Hampton and Mark Clark. In 1984, the Spanish Action Committee of Chicago won a suit against the Chicago Police Department for its violations of civil rights.[24]

The single most deadly act of repression took place during the multiracial Attica prison uprising of 1971, where prisoners were demanding improved conditions. Their rebellion was crushed by a brutal military attack that took forty lives, including those of nine hostages. Southern reporter Tom Wicker of the *New York Times* wrote: "The racial harmony that prevailed among the prisoners—it was absolutely astonishing. . . . That prison yard was the first place I have ever seen where there was no racism."[25]

As the Vietnam War ended and war production declined, the usual economic recessions followed. People scrambled to survive, and the movements for political and economic democracy slowed down. Unemployment increased, and a white backlash gained strength. It helped the radical right gain control of the Republican Party and elect Ronald Reagan to the presidency.

During the presidencies of Reagan and his vice president, George Bush (1981–1993), the federal government gutted the 1975 Voting Rights Act by radically reducing the number of counties required to provide bilingual ballots. As a result, even in Los Angeles County, 35 percent Latino, there was no longer a bilingual ballot. In 1993, the Supreme Court, in a case involving districts redrawn to correct earlier racist tricks, ruled by a 5-to-4 vote that the rights of *white voters* were being unconstitutionally threatened.[26]

Equal economic opportunity became even more unattainable as defense spending skyrocketed and social welfare programs were slashed to the bone. Costly programs like the Strategic Defense Initiative, or "Star Wars," swelled the U.S. federal budget deficit. But this also forced the Soviet Union to spend more than it could afford on defense instead of improving its economy. With the double burden of economic decline and an absence of democracy, Soviet and East European communism collapsed.

The "Reagan free market revolution" of the 1980s generated considerable speculation in stocks and bonds, what commentators called a "casino economy," but little new investment in manufacturing. The deindustrialization of America moved faster, as more factories moved to Mexico and other low-wage havens. Social programs wilted. By the early 1990s, all that was left intact was Head Start—and it was underfunded.

As we saw at the end of the previous chapter, poverty worsened. Crime and drug problems escalated. AIDS and tuberculosis reached epidemic proportions. Homeless people appeared on the nation's sidewalks, asking for spare change.

Once again the white backlash blamed "those people"—usually blacks, Latinos, newly arriving immigrants, or even women since they too came under the rubric of affirmative action. Accusations of "welfare cheats" filled the air. Politicians promised to end welfare and introduce workfare, but no one knew where they would find jobs for the welfare recipients. Hundreds of thousands more workers were laid off as the economy stagnated and the defense industry cut back with the end of the Cold War. As they went for their welfare checks, newly unemployed whites discovered that they could not survive on them.

Fresh outbursts of nativism scapegoated Latino and

other immigrants for "taking American jobs." Actually, few U.S. workers were interested in the jobs the poorest immigrants accepted, as confirmed by INS surveys. As seen in chapter 1, immigrants actually contributed to job creation rather than to job loss and helped keep the economy going. The truth about immigrants was drowned out, however, by a chorus of renewed media distortions.[27]

Immigrants and members of other discriminated-against groups, such as homosexuals, were increasingly attacked.[28] Reports of border shootings of immigrants by border patrol agents and Ku Klux Klansmen increased. San Diego television stations ran special news reports on white suburban teenagers shooting at Mexicans "for sport." In 1991, before the police beating of Rodney King, a special commission investigating police brutality in the Los Angeles Police Department uncovered numerous police car radio messages like "We're huntin wabbits," "I almost got me a Mexican last nite," and "Capture him, beat him and treat him like dirt."[29] A 1991 report by a seventeen-member New York State Judicial Commission on Minorities found "two justice systems at work."[30]

For years, concerned Chicanos in southern California had been videotaping police beatings of Latinos and delivering them to police commanders without results. After King's assailants were acquitted, Los Angeles went up in flames. Half the residents in the hardest-hit neighborhoods were Latino, as were half of those arrested.[31]

For immigrants, there was seldom justice. The world-renowned human rights organization Americas Watch issued a scathing report, "Frontier Justice." It censured the U.S. Justice Department for failing to seriously investigate hundreds of well-documented complaints against the border patrol. In 1993, an INS border patrol agent murdered an unarmed man fleeing across the border and then tried to conceal the body. He was acquitted by a jury in Tucson, Arizona. Pressured by Latinos, the federal government announced a new trial, this time for the agent's violation of the victim's civil rights.

None of this was new to Latino human rights activists. Years earlier, they and leaders of the new unionism organizing immigrant workers (see chapters 1 and 3) had helped draft a *new* Bill of Rights for Undocumented Workers. Proclaimed at an international meeting in Mexico City in 1980, the thirteen articles stated that all immigrant workers:

> *shall have the right to establish legal residency by demonstrating a status as wage earner and taxpayer . . . all of the Constitutional Rights guaranteed all persons in the U.S. . . . all the rights guaranteed to citizen workers including socio-economic and labor rights . . . the right to vote in local and state elections from the moment of legalizing their immigration status.*[32]

After the conference, a campaign was initiated to win fair hearings for detained immigrants. Activists demonstrated regularly at local police headquarters, jails, and detention centers calling for an end to the escalating violence against immigrants. Police departments in Chicago, Santa Ana, San Jose, and other cities agreed not to cooperate with the INS.[33] Unfortunately, the mass media's "brown scare" had more impact.

Meanwhile, Latino organizations like LULAC, MALDEF, the GI Forum, the Cuban National Planning Council, and the San Diego-based Committee on Chicano Rights (CCR) mounted strong opposition to the anti-immigrant Simpson-Mazzoli bill (the 1986 Immigration Reform and Control Act—see chapter 1). As Congress discussed the possibility of a national ID card, LULAC's José Treviño warned that Simpson-Mazzoli would increase "the likelihood of discriminatory actions against Hispanics. It institutes identification practices comparable to Nazi Germany and South Africa."[34] To reduce opposition to the bill, Congress added provisions offering amnesty to any immigrant able to prove continuous residence since 1982 and prohibiting discrimination against Latinos and others on the job market.

But IRCA's sanctions against employers hiring "illegals" badly hurt Latinos. Some employers resented the mountains of paperwork necessary for complying with the new regulations and turned away *all* Latino job applicants. During the first year of IRCA's existence, Hispanic unemployment rates rose faster than those of African Americans. More than one authority on immigration lamented: "The day IRCA became law was a dark one for U.S. democracy."[35]

As Mexico's economy nosedived and immigrants continued to cross over the border, anti-immigrant forces claimed that the proposed North American Free Trade Agreement (NAFTA) would solve the illegal immigrant problem by improving economic conditions in Mexico. Latino and labor activists pointed out that as long as wages in the United States were seven times higher than those in Mexico, immigrants would continue to head for the "golden door"—and U.S. factories would leave for Mexico to exploit cheap labor.

A powerful grassroots campaign against NAFTA brought together environmentalist, peace, and labor organizations in all three NAFTA countries (Canada being the third). These activists became so effective that they earned the respectable name of citizen diplomats. The San Diego–based Border Arts Workshop's *Cafe Urgente* (Emergency Café) went on tour in 1991 to educate people on NAFTA. Like the citizen diplomats, it called for replacing NAFTA with a "continental development program" to rebuild and reenergize all three nations' sputtering economies. After hesitating, Latino politicians joined the NAFTA opposition.

A National Toxics Campaign Fund study concluded in 1991 that *maquiladoras* (2,000 U.S. and other foreign-owned assembly plants in northern Mexico) are "turning the border into a 2,000-mile-long Love Canal." An American

An assembly-line worker in a maquiladora plant of a General Motors subsidiary in Cuauhtémoc, Mexico.

Medical Association report described the border region as "a virtual cesspool and breeding ground for infectious disease." Despite these frightening reports, environmentalist groups divided in 1993. Some of the established organizations backed NAFTA when President Bill Clinton added a pro-environment supplemental agreement to NAFTA. Others concluded that the environmental and labor side agreements were not enforceable, but Congress approved NAFTA by a slim margin of 34 votes.[36]

Another pro-democracy struggle for human rights developed around the plight of 2 million Central Americans fleeing the 1980s' warfare in their homelands and applying for political refugee status here. Ever since the civil rights movement, U.S. immigration law had included political refuge as one of three basic immigration criteria. Yet the INS rounded up thousands of Salvadoran, Guatemalan, Honduran, and Nicaraguan families and detained them in barb-wired camps described by journalists as concentration camps. Latinos and Americas Watch condemned the INS policy.[37]

Authoritarian governments work secretly, keeping the truth from their people. In order for political democracy to function, the public must be truthfully informed. Many Americans had not forgotten the secret machinations of the Nixon administration. Then, only a little more than a decade later, they discovered that they had been deceived again. In televised hearings on the Iran-contragate scandal, they were shocked to discover that the White House had used arms sales to Iran to fund a bloody but unsuccessful invasion of Nicaragua by the contras—as the supporters of the overthrown Nicaraguan dictator were called. Congress had voted against continued aid to the contras. Top government officials stood in open violation of the law.[38]

The televised hearings also revealed a plan to suspend the U.S. Constitution and herd 400,000 protesters into detention camps in the event of a U.S. invasion of

Nicaragua. Then, as if that had not been sufficiently horrifying, in the middle of a much touted "Just Say No" war on drugs, journalists discovered that the U.S. planes flying arms to the contras sometimes returned loaded with cocaine for sale on U.S. city streets to raise more money for the illegal war!

Faced with so much deception on the part of their government, people refused to obey undemocratic rulings. Just as long ago white Americans had helped runaway slaves from the South, an "underground railroad" shepherded fleeing Central American refugees away from the clutches of *la migra* (INS). Staffed by Latino and non-Latino religious activists from all faiths, the 100,000-strong "Sanctuary Movement" was reinforced by marches of hundreds of thousands of Americans protesting the White House's war on Central American pro-democracy movements. Latinos were especially active in this new peace movement. The only exceptions were pro-contra Nicaraguans and Cubans, concentrated in Miami.

During the 1984 summer Olympics in Los Angeles, Latinos conducted an antiwar rally, shouting "Hands Off Nicaragua!" and "Hell No, We Won't Go!" Latino veterans joined the Vietnam Veterans' Convoy of trucks to deliver food to the Nicaraguan people. The new antiwar movement eventually won its goal of ending U.S. aid to the contras and forcing the government to endorse a Central American peace plan. As the U.S.-backed dictatorship in El Salvador defied the peace plan and continued its killing, the Sanctuary Movement won a court case against the INS. It obligated the government to introduce a temporary sanctuary program in 1991 for Salvadorans.[39]

But genuine political democracy still seemed out of reach. Many Americans felt disillusioned by the continued government lies and secrecy. The Bush administration's 1989 invasion of Panama to capture Manuel Noriega, the dictator the U.S. government had earlier helped impose, also drew public protest despite near-universal distaste for

Noriega. Rallies around the nation, often coordinated by Latinos, denounced the use of force instead of negotiation. Especially condemned were U.S. war atrocities like the well-hidden bombing of civilian, noncombatant neighborhoods—so-called "collateral damage." The 1992 Academy Award for Best Documentary was presented to the producers of *The Panama Deception*, documenting the grim events.[40]

As political refugees fled the turmoil in their homelands, the U.S. government opened or slammed the "golden door" according to a morally repugnant double standard based on race, class, and political philosophy. Chileans and Dominicans opposing U.S.-supported dictatorships were turned away.[41] The door slammed even more decisively in the faces of darker-skinned, lower-class Haitians or Central Americans. Yet the door opened for hundreds of thousands of anticommunist Cubans, many light-skinned and middle or upper class. The government's Cuban Refugee Program offered a billion dollars in relocation assistance in the early 1960s. A Cuban exile later recalled: "When you said that you were a Cuban, it sounded like a magic word that opened every door."[42] Before long, Puerto Ricans, other Latinos, and African Americans complained that Cuban refugees were favored on the job market. In the early 1980s, Miami's predominantly black "Liberty City" residents rioted.

In the 1990s, the two most important aspects of democracy—freedom from want and political freedom—remained elusive dreams for most Latinos. They remain disenfranchised by harsh economic circumstances, immigrant status, the absence of bilingual ballots, or unfairly drawn electoral districts.

As we have seen, lack of economic democracy presents a stubborn problem. That is why many Latinos support the new unionism. By percentage of population, there are almost as many Latinos in labor unions as whites (about 1.3 million)—and there are more Latina women in unions than white women.[43]

Poverty remains a terrible blight. Many Americans

hope that this shameful situation can be reversed. With the Cold War over, they want their nation to put people to work at meaningful, fulfilling jobs. There is enough work waiting to be done to provide jobs for decades: building new bridges, housing, railroad tracks, airplanes, improved roads and highways, and cleaning up the environmental mess. The list seems endless.

Latinos, who have contributed so much to the making of America, hope that they can go on playing an important role in rebuilding America and reviving democracy.

SOURCE NOTES

INTRODUCTION

1. The term "Hispanic" became official usage in the 1980 Census. It was introduced in the 1970s as part of a government and commercial effort to "package" Latinos and to depoliticize their energetic empowerment movements. Few Latinos liked the term at the time. It connotes "Spanish," or "Spain," the country against which the ancestors of most Latinos fought for national independence. For more, see chapter 4; also, Rodolfo Acuña, *Occupied America: A History of Chicanos* (New York: HarperCollins, 3d ed., 1988), 379–386.

2. Worldwide, of course, whites are a numerical minority. Some Hispanics are white, but in this book series we include them in the category Latino or Hispanic in order to avoid the awkwardness of "non-Hispanic whites." Unfortunately, none of these skin pigmentation, racial, ethnic, linguistic, and other labels reveal the simple fact that *every* individual is a human being. The term "minority," however, does mean lack of equal power—and that is the scientific way that social scientists use it. Women, for example, even though they slightly outnumber men, are a "minority." In this book we use the term with respect to U.S. society in *both* the numerical and power sense, except when referring to women as a minority.

3. For more, see U.S. Bureau of the Census, *Current*

Population Reports, Washington, D.C.: GPO, 1990–1993, especially Series P20-455, "The Hispanic Population in the United States: March 1991," and P23-183, "Hispanic Americans Today," 1993.

4. People without a piece of paper proving their "legal" right to be here. The term "illegal," like the term "alien," is a negative racial stereotype. A person can *do* an illegal thing, but can a person *be* "illegal"? The term "illegal alien" is doubly negative. There are many reasons people without documents, the "undocumented" (also a negative term), go uncounted. For details, see James D. Cockcroft, *Outlaws in the Promised Land* (New York: Grove, 1988), 14–18, 35–43, 142.

5. Cockcroft, 48–51.

6. For details, see Clara E. Rodríguez, Virginia Sánchez Korrol, and José Oscar Alers, eds., *The Puerto Rican Struggle: Essays on Survival in the U.S.* (Seattle: The Waterfront Press, 1980), 41; Clara E. Rodríguez, *Puerto Ricans Born in the U.S.A.* (Boston: Unwin Hyman, 1989), 98–99. Good overviews are available in Nicolás Kanellos, ed., *The Hispanic-American Almanac* (Detroit: Gale Research, 1993); Edwin Melendez, Clara Rodríguez, and Janis Barry Figueroa, eds., *Hispanics in the Labor Force* (New York: Plenum Press, 1991); Rebecca Morales and Frank Bonilla, eds., *Latinos in a Changing U.S. Economy* (Newbury Park, CA: Sage, 1993); Alfred Stepan, ed., *Americas* (New York: Oxford University Press, 1992).

7. *Encyclopedia Americana* (International Edition, 1964), 653–54.

8. Quoted in Cockcroft, 62.

9. For more, see James D. Cockcroft, *Hispanics in the Struggle for Social Justice* (New York: Franklin Watts, 1994), chapters 2 and 3; Gilberto López y Rivas, *The Chicanos* (New York: Monthly Review Press, 1973), 35.

10. For more, see Morales and Bonilla, 1–26, 127.

11. The job distribution comparisons are for males. The only major difference for Latinas is that more of them

work in services. See Hedda Garza, *Latinas: Hispanic Women in the United States* (New York: Franklin Watts, 1994).

12. For more, see this series' forthcoming *Hispanic Professionals; Hispanics in Politics;* and *Hispanics in the Struggle for Equal Education.*

13. See this series' forthcoming *Hispanics in Film, Stage, and Television; Hispanics in the Art World; Hispanics in the Music World;* and *Hispanic Writers.*

14. Cockcroft, *Outlaws,* 40.

CHAPTER 1

1. Chavez quoted in video "Wrath of Grapes" (La Paz, California: United Farm Workers 1986); Moreno in Rodolfo Acuña, *Occupied America: A History of Chicanos* (New York: HarperCollins, third ed., 1988), 238; Guthrie in James D. Cockcroft, *Outlaws in the Promised Land* (New York: Grove, 1988), 13. The facts in this chapter are drawn largely from Acuña; Cockcroft; and Hedda Garza, *Latinas: Hispanic Women in the United States* (New York: Franklin Watts, 1994).

2. For more on this period of history, see Acuña, 1–130; James D. Cockcroft, *Hispanics in the Struggle for Social Justice* (New York: Franklin Watts, 1994), and *Mexico* (New York: Monthly Review Press, 1990), 58–74; Robert J. Rosenbaum, *Mexicano Resistance in the Southwest* (Austin: University of Texas Press, 1981).

3. For more, see Arnoldo De León, *They Called Them Greasers: Anglo Attitudes Towards Mexicans in Texas, 1821–1900* (Austin: University of Texas Press, 1983).

4. Gilberto López y Rivas, *The Chicanos* (New York: Monthly Review Press, 1973), 34.

5. For more on the "revolving door," see Cockcroft, *Outlaws,* 42–93.

6. Quoted in Cockcroft, *Outlaws,* 22–24.

7. Acuña, 155.

8. By the peak of Wobbly organizing in 1916–1919,

Mexicans from the Agricultural Workers Organization accounted for half of the IWW's total annual dues. See Dan Georgakas, *Solidarity Forever: The IWW Reconsidered* (Chicago: Lakeview Press, 1985), 30–53.

9. Acuña, 184; Cockcroft, *Outlaws,* 57–58. For more on the "brown scares" and immigration laws, see chapters 3 and 6.

10. Acuña, 209.

11. For the moving stories of Latina women in these struggles, see Garza. See also chapter 3; Cockcroft, *Hispanics,* and *Outlaws,* 59–60.

12. Steinbeck apparently knew about the Mexicans' hard lives, but when he wrote about them in his novels *Tortilla Flat* and *Cannery Row* he portrayed them as a bunch of wine-swigging and prostitute "low-lifes."

13. Quoted in Cockcroft, *Outlaws,* 68. For a summation of the bracero program, see Kitty Calavita, *Inside the State: The Bracero Program, Immigration, and the I.N.S.* (New York: Routledge, 1992), 1–17, and Cockcroft, *Outlaws,* 67–88.

14. Quoted in Cockcroft, *Outlaws,* 21–23.

15. The immigrants still call the Rio Grande the "Rio Bravo" (angry river) because, as one old-time bracero explains, "It's gobbled up a lot of Mexicans . . . it has a fish with a beak that bites you in the stomach and empties your guts." Quoted in Cockcroft, *Outlaws,* 33–34 (on Operation Wetback, 78–79).

16. For more, see Garza; Emilio Pantojas-García, *Development Strategies as Ideology: Puerto Rico's Export-Led Industrialization Experience* (Boulder: Lynne Rienner Publishers, 1990).

17. On Huerta and other UFW women, see Garza; also Rosalyn Baxandall, Linda Gordon and Susan Reverby, eds., *America's Working Women* (New York: Random House, 1976), 363–372. On Chavez, Orendain, and the UFW, see Cockcroft, *Outlaws,* 179–189; John Gregory Dunne, *Delano* (New York: Farrar, Straus and Giroux, 1967);

Consuelo Rodriguez, *Cesar Chavez* (New York: Chelsea House, 1991).

18. Author's interviews with returning Vietnam War veterans, 1968–1969.

19. *New York Times,* January 19, 1992; U.S. Census Bureau annual reports. For more, see Frank D. Bean, Barry Edmonston and Jeffrey S. Passel, *Undocumented Immigration to the United States* (Washington, D.C.: The Urban Institute Press, 1990), 222–225; Cockcroft, *Outlaws,* 141, 209–238, 283.

20. An ABC Prime Time television segment, December 2, 1993, revealed the horror. Commentator John Quiñones concluded: "Most people would call this slavery."

21. Ford Foundation, *Hispanics: Challenges and Opportunities* (New York: 1984), 20.

22. Quoted in Cockcroft, *Outlaws,* 41.

23. For details, see Cockcroft, *Outlaws,* 175–208.

24. W. K. Barger and Ernesto M. Reza, *The Farm Labor Movement in the Midwest* (Austin: University of Texas Press, 1993); Kim Moody and Mary McGinn, *Unions and Free Trade: Solidarity vs. Competition* (Detroit: Labor Notes, 1992), 50; Kent Paterson, "Farmworkers," *Coatimundi* (Albuquerque, New Mexico), 2:3 (Summer 1987), 16.

25. Colby made his claim in widely quoted interviews granted to *Playboy* magazine and the *Los Angeles Times* in June 1978—see Cockcroft, *Outlaws,* 39, 259. For more on Simpson-Mazzoli and IRCA, see Cockcroft, *Outlaws,* 209–257.

26. See note 1 above.

CHAPTER 2

1. Quoted in Diane Telgen and Jim Kamp, eds., *Notable Hispanic American Women* (Detroit: Gale Research, 1993), 229. This chapter draws heavily on Hedda Garza, *Women in Medicine* (New York: Franklin Watts, 1994); U.S. Department of Health & Human Services, *Minorities &*

Women in the Health Fields (Washington, D.C.: 1990 ed.) and *Revitalizing Health Professions Education for Minorities and the Disadvantaged* (Washington, D.C.: 1986).

2. 1990 Census, cited by *Diálogo* (Newsletter of National Puerto Rican Policy Network, Summer 1993), 11–12. The figures for every group have been rising slightly since 1990.

3. U.S. Department of Health & Human Services, *Minorities,* 1990, 9, 11, 17, 24, 37, 89, 97.

4. Quoted in U.S. Department of Health & Human Services, *Revitalizing* , 2, 5.

5. For more, see Richard Griswold del Castillo, "The San Ysidro Massacre: A Community Response to Tragedy," *Journal of Borderland Studies,* III:2 (Fall 1988), 65–79; Richard L. Hough et al., "Mental Health Consequences of the San Ysidro McDonald's Massacre: A Community Study," *Journal of Traumatic Stress,* III:1 (1990), 71, 90–91.

6. For more details, see Garza.

7. For more, see Vandana Shiva et al., *Biodiversity* (London: Zed Books, 1991), 43–58, 105–120.

8. Gena Corea. *The Hidden Malpractice* (New York: Harper & Row, 1977), 71.

9. Rivera quote from Sam Roberts, "A New Face for American Labor," *New York Times Magazine,* May 10, 1992, 14. See also, *New York Times,* May 25, 1993; James D. Cockcroft, *Hispanics in the Struggle for Social Justice* (New York: Franklin Watts, 1994); Leon Fink and Leon Greenberg, *Union Power, Soul Power: The Unquiet History of the Hospital Workers* (Urbana: University of Illinois Press, 1989); and Hedda Garza, *Latinas: Hispanic Women in the United States* (New York: Franklin Watts, 1994).

10. U.S. Department of Health and Human Services, *Revitalizing,* 19.

11. For Asians and Asian Americans, it is different. Many of the new immigrants from Asia are already doctors or other professionals.

12. Quoted in U.S. Department of Health & Human

Services, *Revitalizing,* 36. See also U.S. Department of Health & Human Services, *Minorities,* 24–25.

13. Quoted in U.S. Department of Health and Human Services, *Revitalizing,* 6.

14. Quoted in Telgen and Kamp, 349.

15. Author's interviews with participants in Lincoln Hospital struggle, 1979. For more, see Edna Acosta-Belén, *The Puerto Rican Woman* (New York: Praeger, 1986), 14; Cockcroft; Garza, *Latinas* and *Women.*

16. *New York Times,* Aug. 29, 1993; author's interviews with immigrant rights advocates, September, 1993. For more on the "illegals" and how they help build America, see chapters 1 and 3; James D. Cockcroft, *Outlaws in the Promised Land* (New York: Grove, 1988).

CHAPTER 3

1. Howard Zinn, *A People's History of the United States* (New York: HarperPerennial ed., 1990), 226. This chapter is based largely on Rodolfo Acuña, *Occupied America: A History of Chicanos* (New York: HarperCollins, third ed., 1988); James D. Cockcroft, *Hispanics in the Struggle for Social Justice* (New York: Franklin Watts, 1994) and *Outlaws in the Promised Land* (New York: Grove, 1988); Hedda Garza, *Latinas: Hispanic Women in the United States* (New York: Franklin Watts, 1994); Carey McWilliams, *North from Mexico* (New York: Greenwood Press, 1968); Zinn.

2. Quoted in M. B. Schnapper, *American Labor: A Pictorial Social History* (Washington, D.C.: Public Affairs Press, 1975), 146.

3. Quoted in Cockcroft, *Outlaws,* 50.

4. Quoted in McWilliams, 196.

5. Quoted in Victor Clark, *Mexican Labor in the United States* (Washington, D.C.: U.S. Department of Commerce Bulletin No. 79, GPO, 1908), 494.

6. Hubert Howe Bancroft, *History of Arizona and New*

Mexico (San Francisco: The History Co., 1889), quoted in Acuña, 94–95.

7. Quoted in Acuña, 114.

8. Cited in Acuña, 119.

9. James Colquhoun, *The Early History of the Clifton-Morenci District* (London: William Clowes & Sons, Ltd., 1924), 37, 39, 82–83.

10. Mining work is notoriously dangerous and requires both courage and skill. In "block caving" work, the miners deliberately undercut a block of ore to *create* a cave-in to crush the ore and then have it trammed to the hoisting shafts.

11. For more on her and other individual Latina women named in this chapter, see Garza.

12. Zinn, 267.

13. A local historian called it "the bloodiest battle in the history of mining"—quoted in Acuña, 98.

14. For details, see Dan Georgakas, *Solidarity Forever: The IWW Reconsidered* (Chicago: Lakeview Press, 1985), 30–53.

15. Acuña, 174; Cockcroft, *Outlaws*, 39.

16. Chicano Communications Center, *450 Años del Pueblo Chicano: 450 Years of Chicano History in Pictures* (Albuquerque: Chicano Communications Center, 1976), 96; Samuel Yellen, *American Labor Struggles, 1877–1934* (New York: Monad Press, 1936), 205–250; Zinn, 346–349.

17. Acuña, 166. For more, see James D. Cockcroft, *Mexico* (New York: Monthly Review Press, 1990), 110.

18. For the full story, see James D. Cockcroft, *Neighbors in Turmoil: Latin America* (New York: Harper & Row, 1989), 252–254, 278–280 (revised ed., Nelson-Hall, 1994).

19. Quoted in Dan Georgakas, *Solidarity Forever: The IWW Reconsidered* (Chicago: Lakeview Press, 1985), 130–132.

20. Blanche Wiesen Cook, *Eleanor Roosevelt* (New York: Penguin Books, 1992), vol. 1, 250–254.

21. Noted in Cook, vol. 1, 237.

22. Theodore Lothrop Stoddard, *The Rising Tide of Labor Against White World-Supremacy* (New York: C. Scribner's Sons, 1920), 107–108; Remsen Crawford, "The Menace of Mexican Immigration," *Current History*, 31:5 (1930), 905, and C. M. Goethe, "Other Aspects of the Problem," *Current History*, 28:5 (1928), 767.

23. Quoted in Mario T. García, *Mexican Americans* (New Haven: Yale University Press, 1989), 27.

24. *Scribner's Commentary*, in James Jennings and Monte Rivera, eds., *Puerto Rican Politics in Urban America* (Westport: Greenwood Press, 1984), 37.

25. For more on "El Barrio," see Gerald Meyer, *Vito Marcantonio* (Albany: State University of New York Press, 1989), 144–172.

26. For more on the important role of Latinas, see García, 145–237; Garza; Vicki L. Ruiz, *Cannery Women, Cannery Lives: Mexican Women, Unionization, and the California Food Processing Industry, 1930–1950* (Albuquerque: University of New Mexico Press, 1987).

27. For details, see Acuña, 229, and Schnapper, 506–507. A very educational 1993 PBS video series, *The Great Depression*, has live footage of these events.

28. Acuña, 256–160; García, 145–174; McWilliams, 228–258; Mauricio Mazón, *The Zoot-Suit Riots* (Austin: University of Texas Press, 1984).

29. For more, see James Aranson, *The Press and the Cold War* (Indianapolis: Bobbs-Merrill, 1970); Richard M. Freeland, *The Truman Doctrine and the Origins of McCarthyism* (New York: Knopf, 1971); Mary Beth Norton, *A People & A Nation* (Boston: Houghton Mifflin, 1984), vol. B, 434–435; Zinn, 416–428.

30. For more, see Cockcroft, *Outlaws*, 74–75; García, 199–227; Dennis Nodín Valdés, *El Pueblo Mexicano en Detroit y Michigan: A Social History* (Detroit: Wayne State University, 1982), 75–77.

31. Cockcroft, *Outlaws*, 200; Phill Kwik, "The Teamsters Victory: A Successful Strategy for Revitalizing

the Labor Movement," *New Politics,* 4:1 (Summer 1992), 155.

32. For more, see *Guardian,* June 13, 1990, 19; Barbara Kingsolver, *Holding the Line: Women in the Great Arizona Mine Strike of 1983* (Ithaca: ILR Press, Cornell University, 1989), ix, 192–195; *New York Times,* March 19 and 23, 1986.

CHAPTER 4

1. Quoted in Shirley Achor, *Mexican Americans in a Dallas Barrio* (Tucson: University of Arizona Press, 1978), 94, and James Diego Vigil, *Barrio Gangs* (Austin: University of Texas Press, 1988), 60. Unless otherwise indicated, the information for this chapter is drawn from James D. Cockcroft, *Hispanics in the Struggle for Social Justice* (New York: Franklin Watts, 1994); Hedda Garza, *Latinas: Hispanic Women in the United States* (New York: Franklin Watts, 1994); Jonathan Kozol, *Savage Inequalities* (New York: Crown, 1991); Joan Moore and Harry Pachon, *Hispanics in the United States* (Englewood Cliffs: Prentice-Hall, 1985), 66–70, 145–158; Guadalupe San Miguel, Jr., "Education," in Nicolás Kanellos, *The Hispanic-American Almanac* (Detroit: Gale Research, 1993), 287–307.

2. This scene is condensed from a chapter by Eugene Bucchioni in Francesco Cordasco and Eugene Bucchioni, eds., *The Puerto Rican Experience* (Totowa: Rowman and Littlefield, 1973), 279–300. The dialogue in the teachers' room is from pages 293–294, and all names are fictitious.

3. Quoted in Kal Wagenheim and Olga Jiménez de Wagenheim, *The Puerto Ricans* (New York: Praeger Publishers, 1973), 309.

4. Mrs. Clementina Castro, quoted in Milwaukee County Welfare Rights Organization, Thomas Howard Tarantino and Rev. Dismas Becker, eds., *Welfare Mothers Speak Out* (New York: W. W. Norton, 1972), 70–71.

5. For more, see Garza; Adalberto López and James

Petras, eds., *Puerto Rico and Puerto Ricans: Studies in History and Society* (Cambridge: Schenkman, 1974), 327–328; Virginia E. Sánchez Korrol, *From Colonia to Community* (Westport: Greenwood Press, 1983), 75–76, 156.

6. Quoted in Odie B. Faulk, *Land of Many Frontiers* (New York: Oxford University Press, 1968), 318.

7. San Miguel, Jr., in Kanellos, 298. By 1900, only New Mexico, where Anglos were a minority, still allowed the use of Spanish in school. For more, see Mario T. García, *Desert Immigrants: the Mexicans of El Paso 1880–1920* (New Haven: Yale University Press, 1981), 124–125; Moore and Pachon, 145–149; David Montejano, *Anglos and Mexicans in the Making of Texas, 1836–1986* (Austin: University of Texas Press, 1987), 157–256.

8. Kanellos, 238.

9. For more on Lemon Grove, see Robert R. Alvarez, "National Politics and Local Responses: the Nation's First Successful School Desegregation Case," in Henry Trueba and Concha Delgado-Gaitan, eds., *Schooling and Society: Learning Content Through Culture* (New York: Praeger Publishers, 1988), 37–52.

10. See Rodolfo Acuña, *Occupied America: A History of Chicanos* (New York: Harper & Row, third ed., 1988), 236–241, 294–295. For a history of LULAC through the 1980s, see Richard A. Garcia, *Rise of the Mexican American Middle Class*, 252–322. For the 1929–1960 period see Mario T. García, *Mexican Americans* (New Haven: Yale University Press, 1989), 25–61.

11. Acuña, 289–290, and Mario T. García, *Mexican*, 56–58 and 89–91.

12. Mario T. García, *Mexican*, 59–61; photo in Kanellos, 388.

13. President Lyndon Johnson, 1965, quoted in David J. Garrow, *Bearing the Cross* (New York: Vintage Books, 1988), 408.

14. For details, see Hedda Garza, *Joan Baez* (New York: Chelsea House, 1991), 26–29.

15. For more, see Cockcroft, *Hispanics.* Also, Acuña, ix; Richard Griswold del Castillo, *The Treaty of Guadalupe Hidalgo: A Legacy of Conflict* (Norman: University of Oklahoma Press, 1990), 146–153; Armando B. Rendon, *Chicano Manifesto* (New York: The Macmillan Company, 1971), 119–131.

16. For more on Chicana women in the Brown Berets, consult Garza, *Latinas.* On blow-outs, see Carlos Muñoz, Jr., *Youth, Identity, Power* (New York: Verso, 1989), 64–68.

17. Noted in Rebecca Morales and Frank Bonilla, eds., *Latinos in a Changing U.S. Economy* (Newbury Park: Sage, 1993), 42; see also, Gary D. Sandefur and Marta Tienda, *Divided Opportunities* (New York: Plenum Press, 1988), 194.

18. Cordasco and Bucchioni, 315. See also, Clara E. Rodríguez, Virginia Sánchez Korrol, and José Oscar Alers, eds., *The Puerto Rican Struggle: Essays on Survival in the U.S.* (Maplewood: The Waterfront Press, 1980), 111–120.

19. The Kansas City story is based on author's interviews with "Elena," October, 1993.

20. Kozol, 59–60.

21. Quoted in *New York Teacher,* June 14, 1993.

22. Quoted in *New York Teacher,* June 14, 1993. On the Cubans' bilingual program and later Latino ones, see Felix M. Padilla, *Puerto Rican Chicago* (Notre Dame, Indiana: University of Notre Dame Press, 1987), 212. On ESL dropoff and increase in LEP students, see *Hispanic,* September 1993, 62; Alfred Stepan, ed., *Americas* (New York: Oxford University Press, 1992), 302.

23. For details, see 1980 and 1990 Censuses; Edward M. Chen, "Today's Immigrants Learn English as Fast as Yesterday's Did," *New York Times,* Sept. 29, 1989, citing a 1985 Rand Corporation study and other research; Morales and Bonilla, 239; Stepan, 290–303.

24. Quoted in Kozol, 218; for more on this question in Texas and other states, see 214–221, 223–229.

25. *New York Teacher,* June 14, 1993; see also, chapters 5 and 6.

26. For more, see Kozol, 206–233; Acuña, 386–393.

27. Quoted in Guadalupe San Miguel, Jr., *Let All of Them Take Heed* (Austin: University of Texas Press, 1987), 170. On Puerto Rican organizations relating to education, see Francesco Cordasco, ed. *The Puerto Ricans 1493–1973* (Dobbs Ferry: Oceana Publications, 1973), 13–16; Cordasco and Bucchioni, 279–354.

28. Author's interviews with founders of Workers University from the Dominican Republic and Ecuador.

29. Gregory DeFreitas, *Inequality at Work* (New York: Oxford University Press, 1991), 205; *The Chronicle of Higher Education,* March 18, 1992; *Hispanic,* September 1993, 62, 64.

30. The estimate on hunger is the lowest one reported—some estimates go as high as 30 million. The more advantaged Cubans show 17.2 percent with college degrees, almost the same as whites. See tables in Moore and Pachon, 68, 70, and Edwin Melendez, Clara Rodriguez and Janis Barry Figueroa, eds., *Hispanics in the Labor Force* (New York: Plenum Press, 1991), 10–12.

31. See Melendez, Rodriguez and Figueroa, 53–75.

32. *The Daily Astorian,* May 28, 1993.

33. Kozol, 3. On African Americans, see Clarence Lusane, *The Struggle for Equal Education* (New York: Franklin Watts, 1992).

34. Linda Chavez, *Out of the Barrio* (New York: Basic Books, 1991), 163.

35. Hero, 167; *New York Times,* January 25, May 23, November 15, 1993.

36. New York State Social Studies Review and Development Committee, *One Nation, Many Peoples: A Declaration of Cultural Interdependence* (Albany: New York State Education Department, 1991).

37. On California, see Kozol, 221. In meetings attended by several leading educators, this author has noticed that many of them express these views more in private than in public.

CHAPTER 5

1. Quoted in Felix M. Padilla, *Puerto Rican Chicago* (Notre Dame: University of Notre Dame Press, 1987), 234. Documentation for this chapter may be found in Nicolás Kanellos, ed., *The Hispanic-American Almanac* (Detroit: Gale Research Inc., 1993). For more on Latinas in the professions, politics, business, and the arts, see Hedda Garza, *Latinas: Hispanic Women in the United States* (New York: Franklin Watts, 1994), and Diane Telgen and Jim Kamp, eds., *Notable Hispanic American Women* (Detroit: Gale Research Inc., 1993).

2. For more on this, see Susan Faludi, *Backlash* (New York: Crown, 1991); Garza; Kanellos, 344–345; Edwin Melendez, Clara Rodriguez and Janis Barry Figueroa, eds., *Hispanics in the Labor Force* (New York: Plenum Press, 1991), 6–20; Rebecca Morales and Frank Bonilla, eds., *Latinos in a Changing U.S. Economy* (Newbury Park: Sage, 1993), 1–36, 91.

3. U.S. Bureau of the Census. *Current Population Reports,* P20–455, "The Hispanic Population in the United States: March 1991" (Washington, D.C.: GPO, 1991), 2.

4. Quoted in Kanellos, 242.

5. Quoted in *New York Times,* July 8, 1993. For more on Latinos in law and politics, see Acuña, 415–425; Kanellos, 229–286; Harry Pachon and Louis DeSipio, "Latino Elected Officials in the 1990s," *PS: Political Science and Politics,* June 1992, 213.

6. Kanellos, 676; see also chapter 2.

7. Quoted in Telgen and Kamp, 373.

8. U.S. Bureau of the Census, "1987 Survey of Minority-Owned Businesses," *Census and You* (Washington, D.C.: GPO, August 1991), 10.

9. Quoted in Joe Vidueira, "Thumbs Down," *Hispanic,* November 1993, 46, 48.

10. Five Latino veterans—Roberto Alomar, Bobby Bonilla, Jose Canseco, Rubin Sierra, and Danny Tartabull—

are among the twenty highest-paid players. See Milton Jamail, "Major League Bucks," *Hispanic,* April 1993, 18.

11. Quoted in Kanellos, 550.

12. Quoted in Kanellos, 555.

13. Quoted in *Hispanic,* March 1992, 12.

14. Quoted in *Hispanic,* March 1992, 14.

15. Richard Rodriguez, *Hunger of Memory* (Boston: David R. Godine, 1982), 151.

16. Quoted in *Hispanic,* December 1991, 15. For more, see Eva Cockcroft, John Weber, and James Cockcroft, *Toward a People's Art: The Contemporary Mural Movement* (New York: E. P. Dutton, 1977); James D. Cockcroft, *Diego Rivera* (New York: Chelsea House, 1991); Hedda Garza, *Frida Kahlo* (New York: Chelsea House, 1993).

17. For details, see Garza, *Latinas.*

18. See Hedda Garza, *Pablo Casals* (New York: Chelsea House, 1993).

19. For more on Latinos in music, see: Ronald D. Arroyo, "La Raza Influence in Jazz," in Octavio Ignacio Romano-V., ed., *Voices* (Berkeley: Quinto Sol, 1973), 200–204; Kanellos, 595–619; Padilla, 233–237.

20. Kanellos, 342–343; see also footnote 2.

21. Quoted in Mario T. García, *Mexican Americans* (New Haven: Yale University Press, 1989), 222.

22. *New York Times,* September 4 and 15, 1988, March 23, 1989.

23. For details, see Morales and Bonilla.

24. Kanellos, 350; U.S. Bureau of the Census, *Current Population Reports,* P20–455, 8.

25. See *New York Times,* September 4, 1988; Bettina Gerch, "The Resurrection of Out-Work," *Monthly Review,* November 1985, 37–46.

26. *Diálogo* (Newsletter of National Puerto Rican Policy Network, Summer 1993), 11–12.

27. Nancy Foner, ed., *New Immigrants in New York* (New York: Columbia University Press, 1987), 103–126; Sherri Grasmuck and Patricia R. Pessar, *Between Two Islands*

(Berkeley: University of California Press, 1991), 162–198; Alfred Stepan, ed., *Americas* (New York: Oxford University Press, 1992), 298–299.

28. For details on this myth, see James D. Cockcroft, *Latinos in the Struggle for Social Justice* (New York: Franklin Watts, 1994); Hedda Garza *Latinas* (New York: Franklin Watts, 1994).

CHAPTER 6

1. Quoted in *The Encyclopedia Americana* (International ed., 1964), 538. The main sources of information for this chapter are Rodolfo Acuña, *Occupied America: A History of Chicanos* (New York: Harper & Row, third ed., 1988); James D. Cockcroft, *Hispanics in the Struggle for Social Justice* (New York: Franklin Watts, 1994); Mario T. García, *Mexican Americans* (New Haven: Yale University Press, 1989); Hedda Garza, *Latinas: Hispanic Women in the United States* (New York: Franklin Watts, 1994); Howard Zinn, *A People's History of the United States* (New York: HarperPerennial ed., 1990).

2. Quoted in *The Encyclopedia Americana* (1964 ed.), 549–550.

3. Quoted in James D. Cockcroft, *Neighbors in Turmoil: Latin America* (New York: Harper & Row, 1989), 252 (revised ed., Chicago: Nelson-Hall, 1994).

4. Marcantonio was also a founder of the American Labor Party (ALP), which helped elect the country's first Puerto Rican officeholder, Oscar García Rivera, to the New York State Assembly in 1937. For more, see Gerald Meyers, *Vito Marcantonio* (Albany: State University of New York Press, 1989), 144–172.

5. For more, see Joan Moore and Harry Pachon, *Hispanics in the United States* (Englewood Cliffs: Prentice-Hall, Inc., 1985), 177–178.

6. After the decision, Hernández was tried again,

pleaded guilty, and received a twenty-year sentence. For the full story, see Acuña, 292, and García, 49–51.

7. Shirley Achor, *Mexican Americans in a Dallas Barrio* (Tucson: University of Arizona Press, 1978), 105–106.

8. For more, see García, 25–61; Garza; Benjamín Márquez, *LULAC* (Austin: University of Texas Press, 1993).

9. For more on ANMA, see Garcia, 199–227. For "Red-baiting" of Mexican immigrants, see Kitty Calavita, *Inside the State* (New York: Routledge, Chapman and Hall, 1992), 50–55.

10. Quoted in Nicolás Kanellos, ed., *The Hispanic-American Almanac* (Detroit: Gale Research Inc., 1993), 602, see also 39, 727.

11. Quoted in Virginia E. Sánchez Korrol, *From Colonia to Community* (Westport: Greenwood Press, 1983), 189.

12. On Ríos's election, see Kal Wagenheim and Olga Jimínez de Wagenheim, *The Puerto Ricans* (New York: Praeger Publishers, 1973), 258–263.

13. For more on the GI Forum, CSO, and other civil rights organizations of this period, see Acuña, 253 and 283–293; García, 19, 101–103; Adalberto López and James Petras (eds.), *Puerto Rico and Puerto Ricans* (New York: John Wiley & Sons, 1974), 313–451; Felix M. Padilla, *Puerto Rican Chicago* (Notre Dame: University of Notre Dame Press, 1987), 78–143; Dennis Nodín Valdés, *El Pueblo Mexicano en Detroit y Michigan: A Social History* (Detroit: Wayne State University, 1982), 75–77.

14. For more, see Garza; also, Frances Fox Piven and Richard A. Cloward, *Poor People's Movements* (New York: Vintage Books, 1979), 264–359.

15. Quoted in Padilla, 147.

16. For details and photographs, see *Report of the National Advisory Commission on Civil Disorders* (New York: Bantam, 1968).

17. Acuña, 346; *Hispanic*, August 1993, 36.

18. Anonymous mother, interview with author, June 1971.

19. Zinn, 455, 543.

20. Acuña, 346–350.

21. For more complete information, see Stephen E. Ambrose, *Nixon* (New York: Touchstone, 1991); Hedda Garza, *The Watergate Investigation Index* (Wilmington: Scholarly Resources, 1984).

22. This is the considered assessment of historian Robert J. Goldstein in his *Political Repression in Modern America, from 1870 to Present* (Cambridge: Schenkman, 1978), 429. See also, Acuña, 342–344, 350–352; Zinn, 453, 455.

23. See Clara E. Rodríguez, Virginia Sánchez Korrol, and José Oscar Alers, eds., *The Puerto Rican Struggle: Essays on Survival in the U.S.* (Maplewood: The Waterfront Press, 1980), 127–128; Richard Griswold del Castillo, *The Treaty of Guadalupe Hidalgo: A Legacy of Conflict* (Norman: University of Oklahoma Press, 1990), 144.

24. Padilla, 165–179, 250.

25. Quoted in Zinn, 511.

26. For more, see Moore and Pachon, 169–199; *New York Times,* June 29, 1993.

27. A bone-chilling compilation of racist media bashing of the immigrants may be found in Celestino Fernandez, "The Border Patrol and News Media Coverage of Undocumented Mexican Immigration During the 1970s," *California Sociologist,* 5 (1982). See also Acuña, 371–376.

28. A 1993 research report to the Ford Foundation attributed the increased number of "hate crimes" to a shrinking job market. See Robert L. Bach et al., *Changing Relations* (New York: Ford Foundation, 1993).

29. The head of the commission was Warren M. Christopher, later appointed U.S. Secretary of State. For the police messages, see *New York Times,* July 10, 1991.

30. Quoted in *New York Times,* June 5, 1991.

31. Octavio Emilio Nuiry, "King of the Barrio,"

Hispanic, April 1993, 26–32; *New York Times,* May 29, 1992; author's interviews with Chicano human rights activists, June 1992.

32. For full text, see Cockcroft, *Outlaws,* 281–282.

33. Cockcroft, *Outlaws,* 201; *New York Times,* May 31, 1992; *Washington Post,* May 14, 1993.

34. Quoted in Cockcroft, *Outlaws,* 230. See also chapter 1 and its note 25.

35. Cockcroft, *Outlaws,* 256; for more, see 141, 209–238, 254, 283; also Frank D. Bean, Barry Edmonston, and Jeffrey S. Passel, *Undocumented Immigration to the United States* (Washington, D.C.: The Urban Institute Press, 1990), 222–225, and Rebecca Morales and Frank Bonilla, eds., *Latinos in a Changing U.S. Economy* (Newbury Park: Sage, 1993), 92.

36. *New York Times,* Oct. 12, 1993; author's participation at *"Cafe Urgente,"* Hall Walls, Buffalo, New York, Aug. 16, 1991. For more on NAFTA, see John Cavanagh et al., eds., *Trading Freedom: How Free Trade Affects Our Lives, Work, and Environment* (San Francisco: Food First Books, 1992); Nora Lustig et al., eds., *North American Free Trade: Assessing the Impact* (Washington, D.C.: The Brookings Institution, 1992); Kim Moody and Mary McGinn, *Unions and Free Trade: Solidarity vs. Competition* (Detroit: Labor Notes, 1992).

37. For more, see Cockcroft, *Neighbors,* 60–61, and *Outlaws,* 173, 242–252.

38. For the full story, see James D. Cockcroft, *Daniel Ortega* (New York: Chelsea House, 1991).

39. For background and details, see Cockcroft, *Ortega,* 75–97, and *Neighbors,* 55–62; Ann Crittenden, *Sanctuary* (New York: Weidenfeld & Nicolson, 1988).

40. For more complete information see Cockcroft, *Hispanics,* chapter 7, and *Neighbors,* 52, 211–226. According to most independent investigations, including those mentioned in the 1992 Academy Award Best Documentary *The Panama Deception,* the goal of the invasion was to reassert

U.S. control over Central America and restore to power the traditional "twenty families" that had ruled Panama prior to 1968. This assured Washington that in the year 2000, when the 1977–1978 Canal Treaties' would give Panama sovereignty over the Panama Canal, the "right" people, friendly to U.S. banks and corporations, would be in charge.

41. On the "double standard," see table in Mark Gibney, ed., *Open Borders? Closed Societies? The Ethical and Political Issues* (Westport: Greenwood Press, 1988), 161. For more on U.S. policy in Chile, see Hedda Garza, *Salvador Allende* (New York: Chelsea House, 1989).

42. Quoted in Rodolfo Rodríguez Zaldívar and Bienvenido Madan, *Golden Pages of the Cuban Exiles, 1959–1983* (self-published), 148.

43. Kanellos, 334.

BIBLIOGRAPHY

*Books especially recommended for students.

Acosta-Belén, Edna, and Barbara R. Sjostrom, eds. *The Hispanic Experience in the United States.* New York: Praeger, 1986.
*Acuña, Rodolfo. *Occupied America: A History of Chicanos.* New York: Harper & Row, third ed., 1988.
Barger, W. K., and Ernesto M. Reza. *The Farm Labor Movement in the Midwest.* Austin: University of Texas Press, 1993.
*Chicano Communications Center. *450 Anos del Pueblo Chicano: 450 Years of Chicano History in Pictures.* Albuquerque: Chicano Communications Center, 1976.
*Cockcroft, James D. *Neighbors in Turmoil: Latin America.* New York: Harper & Row, 1989, revised ed., Nelson-Hall, 1994.
*_____. *Hispanics in the Struggle for Social Justice.* New York: Franklin Watts, 1994.
_____. *Mexico.* New York: Monthly Review Press, 1990.
*_____. *Outlaws in the Promised Land.* New York: Grove, 1988.
Cordasco, Francesco, and Eugene Bucchioni, eds. *The Puerto Rican Experience.* Totowa: Rowman and Littlefield, 1973.
*Ford Foundation. *Hispanics: Challenges and Opportunities.* New York: 1984.

García, Mario T. *Mexican Americans*. New Haven: Yale University Press, 1989.

*Garza, Hedda. *Latinas: Hispanic Women in the United States*. New York: Franklin Watts, 1994.

*_____. *Women in Medicine*. New York: Franklin Watts, 1994.

Grasmuck, Sherri, and Patricia R. Pessar. *Between Two Islands*. Berkeley: University of California Press, 1991.

Griswold del Castillo, Richard. *The Treaty of Guadalupe Hidalgo: A Legacy of Conflict*. Norman: University of Oklahoma Press, 1990.

Heyman, Josiah McC. *Life and Labor on the Border: Working People of Northeastern Sonora, Mexico, 1886–1986*. Tucson: University of Arizona Press, 1991.

Kanellos, Nicolás, ed., *The Hispanic-American Almanac*. Detroit: Gale Research Inc., 1993.

*Kozol, Jonathan. *Savage Inequalities: Children in America's Schools*. New York: Crown, 1991.

*Leggett, John C., ed. *Mining the Fields: Farm Workers Fight Back*. Highland Park: Raritan Institute, 1991.

McWilliams, Carey. *North from Mexico*. New York: Greenwood Press, 1968.

Melendez, Edwin, Clara Rodriguez, and Janis Barry Figueroa, eds., *Hispanics in the Labor Force*. New York: Plenum Press, 1991.

Meyer, Gerald. *Vito Marcantonio*. Albany: State University of New York Press, 1989.

Montejano, David. *Anglos and Mexicans in the Making of Texas, 1836–1986*. Austin: University of Texas Press, 1987.

*Moore, Joan, and Harry Pachon, *Hispanics in the United States*. Englewood Cliffs: Prentice-Hall, 1985.

Morales, Rebecca, and Frank Bonilla, eds. *Latinos in a Changing U.S. Economy*. Newbury Park: Sage, 1993.

Padilla, Felix M. *Puerto Rican Chicago*. Notre Dame: University of Notre Dame Press, 1987.

Rodríguez, Clara E., Virginia Sánchez Korrol, and José Oscar Alers, eds. *The Puerto Rican Struggle: Essays on*

Survival in the U.S. Maplewood: The Waterfront Press, 1980.

Ruiz, Vicki L. *Cannery Women, Cannery Lives: Mexican Women, Unionization, and the California Food Processing Industry, 1930–1950.* Albuquerque: University of New Mexico Press, 1987.

Sánchez Korrol, Virgina E. *From Colonia to Community.* Westport: Greenwood Press, 1983.

*Schnapper, M. B. *American Labor: A Pictorial Social History.* Washington, D.C.: Public Affairs Press, 1975.

Stepan, Alfred, ed. *Americas.* New York: Oxford University Press, 1992.

U.S. Bureau of the Census. *Current Population Reports,* P23–183, "Hispanic Americans Today." Washington, D.C.: GPO, 1993.

Wagenheim, Kal, and Olga Jimínez de Wagenheim, *The Puerto Ricans* New York: Praeger Publishers, 1973.

*Weisman, Alan (text), and Jay Dusard (photographs). *La Frontera: The United States Border with Mexico.* New York: Harcourt Brace Jovanovich, 1986.

*Zinn, Howard. *A People's History of the United States.* New York: HarperPerennial ed., 1990.

FILMS/VIDEOS

Año Nuevo. On "undocumented" farm workers' unionizing.

Ballad of an Unsung Hero. Injustice done to a Mexican immigrant.

El Norte. On Guatemalan refugees in U.S.

The Golden Cage: A Story of California's Farmworkers.

The Great Depression. 1993 PBS video series on 1930s.

Growing up Hispanic.

Here to Stay: Young Immigrants from El Salvador.

Los Mineros. 1991 PBS video on miners, including Arizona 1903.

Los Sures. On a Brooklyn barrio.

Manos a la Obra: The Story of Operation Bootstrap.

Migra. On arrest of "undocumented" workers.

New Harvest, Old Shame. PBS, 1990.

The Nine Nations of North America: Mexamerica. PBS, 1988.

Our Hispanic Heritage.

The Panama Deception. 1992 Academy Award winner.

Portrait of Castro's Cuba. PBS, 1991, narrator James Earl Jones.

Puerto Rico: A Colony the American Way.

Salt of the Earth. On famous strike and women's victory.

Who's Running This War? PBS, 1986, on Central America warfare.

Wrath of Grapes. 1986, farmworkers' campaign against pesticides.

Yo Soy (I Am). On Chicanos.

INDEX

Italicized pages numbers refer to illustrations.

Musicians, 131–132
Mutualistas, 67, 68, 123

National Welfare Rights Organization (NWRO), 148
Nativism, 16, 73–74, 154–155
"New unionism," 38, 85–87
Nicaragua, 159–160
Nixon, Richard, 151, 152, 159
Noriega, Manuel, 160–161
North American Free Trade Agreement (NAFTA), 157, 159
Novello, Dr. Antonia, 52, *53*
Nurses, Latino, 46–48, 52, 54

Operation Bootstrap, 31, 83–84
"Operation Wetback" (1954), 29, *30*, 83, 144, 145
Orendain, Tony, 32, 36

Panama, U.S. invasion of, 160–161
Peña, Federico, 116–117
Pesticides, 31, 34, 38, *39*, 40–41
Physicians, 46–48, 52, 54
Piñero, Miguel, 124
PLM (Mexican Liberal Party), 42, 69, 142
Police abuse, 98, 148, 153, 155
Political democracy, 138–139, 143–145, 150–155, 159
Politicians, 15, 116–117
Poor People's Encampment, 150
Poverty, Latinos and, 19, 25, 45–46, 56, 87, 108, 133–135, 138, 154, 161–162. *See also* Economic democracy
Powell, Adam Clayton, *147*
Professionals, 15, 114–115. *See also under specific professions*

Puerto Rican Legal Defense and Education Fund, 115–116
Puerto Ricans, 11–12, 13, 25, 29, 31, 72–73, 76–77, 83–84, 92–93, 98, 100, 108, 124, 134–135, 140, 146, 152–153
Puerto Rico, 55, 73, 94, 109–110. *See also* Operation Bootstrap

Racism, Latinos and, 21, 31, 52, 54, 59, 75, 76, 81, 89, 90–93, 109, 117, 119, 140, 142–143, 155–156. *See also* Brown scares; Stereotyping
Railroad workers, 64, *66*, 67
Rain forest, 49
Reagan, Ronald, 85, 109, 117, 133, 153, 159–160
"Revolving door," 22, *24*, 29, 34–35, 76
Rivera, Dennis, 50, *51*, 52, 85
Rockefeller, John D., 70, 72
Rodriguez, Demetrio, 105
Rodriguez, Dr. Helen, 55
Rodriguez, Juan (Chi), 122
Rodriguez, Richard, 128–129
Roosevelt, Franklin, 11, 80, 138
Roosevelt, Franklin, Jr., *147*
Rosselló, Pedro, 110
Roybal, Edward R., 145
Ruiz, Virginia, 133

Sanctuary Movement, 160
Scapegoating of Latinos, 14, 29, 61, 67, 72, 76–77, 84–85
Scientists and engineers, 117–118
Service workers, 15, 31
South Americans, 11–12, 134

ABOUT THE AUTHOR

Described by the American Library Association's *Choice* magazine as "an internationally known and distinguished scholar," Professor James Cockcroft is also a writer, editor, consultant, and college teacher. The author of more than twenty books on Hispanics, Mexico, immigration, minorities, and international affairs, he has been a Fulbright Scholar three times, a Ford Fellow and Peace Corps consultant, and a 1988 University of California Regents Lecturer. James Cockcroft's recent book for Franklin Watts is *The Hispanic Struggle for Social Justice*.